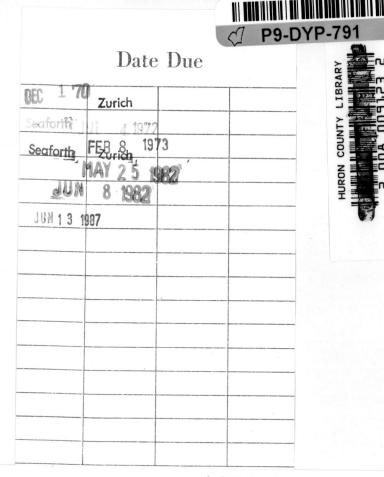

Date Due

DEC 1 70 Zurich		
Seaforth JUL 4 1972		
Seaforth FEB 8 1973 Zurich		
MAY 2 5 1982		
JUN 8 1982		
JUN 1 3 1987		

THE MOUNTIES PATROL THE SEA

THE MOUNTIES PATROL THE SEA

by TOM E. CLARKE

THE WESTMINSTER PRESS · PHILADELPHIA

STANDARD BOOK NO. 664-32445-2

LIBRARY OF CONGRESS CATALOG CARD NO. 69-16302

CREDITS

City Archives, City Hall, Vancouver, Canada: 101 (map),
103–106; Vancouver Maritime Museum: 99, 100, 102

PUBLISHED BY THE WESTMINSTER PRESS®
PHILADELPHIA, PENNSYLVANIA

PRINTED IN THE UNITED STATES OF AMERICA

We left our horses far behind,
And took to the open sea,
For we are the men of the Horse Marines,
But they call us the RCMP.

(Item in Vancouver, B.C., newspaper upon the launching of the *St. Roch*)

Author's Note

I DID NOT WORK ALONE in the production of this book. Without the cooperation of many helpful people the full story of the *St. Roch* could not have been told. I wish, therefore, to express my appreciation to those who devoted time and effort to make the story complete.

Thanks to Jack and Siddie Foster, William J. "Dad" Parry, Staff Sergeant John Friederich, and Major J. S. Matthews for their sharp, clear reminiscences of long-past happenings. Miss Yvonne H. Stevenson, former secretary to the commander of the Victoria subdivision of the R.C.M.P., helped locate persons to be interviewed. Mrs. Adele Case, secretary to David E. Wallace, General Manager of Burrard Dry Dock Company, Ltd., North Vancouver, furnished construction and historical data in reference to the *St. Roch*.

Alfred W. Wills, retired Foreman Shipwright and Dockmaster of Burrard Dry Dock Company, who worked as a shipwright during the building of the ship, gave invaluable details of her construction. The Maritime Museum at Vancouver permitted my inspection of the *St. Roch,* and A. R. "Fred" Douglas furnished old photographs. I am grateful also to Inspector W. R. Pilkey, liaison officer at R.C.M.P. Headquarters, Ottawa, for providing copies of official documents.

7

My only regret is that the project did not begin in time for me to have known Henry Larsen personally. But from talking to those who did know him well, I feel I can agree with John Friederich, who said, "He was a fabulous man!"

[1]

TWO SHIPMASTERS stood looking up at a partly built schooner on the ways of the Burrard Dry Dock Company at North Vancouver, British Columbia. A sharp March wind blew off the steep, wooded mountains behind the city whistling through the open framework of the building shed and flapping the canvas covering. Captain W. H. Gillen, a ruddy Nova Scotian in his sixties, spoke to his husky, fair-haired companion. "What do you think of her?"

Young Captain Henry Larsen squinted blue eyes against the wind. "Round as an egg." The words carried a thick Norwegian accent. "She'll be a great one in the ice, but wicked on the open sea."

"About the only time she'll be in heavy swells will be crossing the Gulf of Alaska and in the Bering Sea."

"I've taken some awful pastings in the Arctic Ocean, Cap."

"So have I, but she'll be frozen in nine months each year, and during open navigation she'll be in the pack most of the time. You know as well as I that they built her round so ice pressure will squeeze her up out of the water and not cave her in."

"Yah, she will be good for ice, all right."

"They're putting only the best of everything into her. Look how thick that planking is, and you should see her frames. Everything is oversize, and the knees all have natural bends for strength. This is the strongest wooden hull ever built in this yard or maybe any yard, for all I know."

Larsen waved toward some long boxes nearby with steam seeping from them. "What are they cooking in the steam boxes?"

"Ironbark. When she's caulked, they'll sheath her from guard to keel with strips an inch and a half thick."

"Ice won't chew through that very easy."

"She'll have steel plates on the bow, too."

"The R.C.M.P. must have great plans for her."

"Didn't Corporal Pasley tell you how they're going to use her?"

"In his letter he yust said the Mounted Police were building a schooner to patrol the Western Arctic, and he's to be in charge of her. He said if I yoin the Force I can be her navigator."

"You were up there long enough to know what's ahead."

"Yah. Where do you fit into the picture, Cap?"

"A civilian engineer and I will take her to Herschel Island and turn her over to the R.C.M.P. inspector commanding the Western Arctic. The rest of the crew will be Mounties."

"You say they're going to leave her up there every winter?"

"She'll come out every few years for refitting, but the rest of the time she'll be a floating R.C.M.P. detachment. During open season she'll patrol and carry supplies to the detachments on the Arctic coast and islands. After freeze-up the crew will operate as regular Mounties, making patrols by sled and dog team."

"How far east will she go?"

"To Cambridge Bay, Victoria Land. You must have been all through there when you were Klingenberg's mate."

"Yah, we put the *Old Maid* into every bay from the Beaufort Sea to Queen Maud Gulf. Anywhere there was a trapper with furs to trade, we went." He eyed the vessel. "About a hundred feet long, eh?"

"A hundred and four. She's got a twenty-five-foot beam and will draw thirteen feet when loaded." Gillen nodded toward the stern. "Let's go aft so you can see the rudder."

They picked their way around the blocks on which the keel was resting, ducking under the framing and timbers that held the vessel upright. Underfoot, the ways were cluttered with chips and shavings and other debris of a wooden vessel's building. Larsen inhaled deeply the scent of newly sawed and adzed timbers of seasoned fir of which the ship was framed and planked. The aroma of linseed oil putty was in the wind too, and the pungent smell of pine tar in the oakum being horsed into seams by two elderly caulkers on a scaffold overhead. The thudding of their mallets rang through the hull and echoed from another ship being built nearby. Reaching the stern, Gillen and Larsen examined the wooden rudder. "Solid ironbark," Gillen said.

Larsen pushed against the rudder, but couldn't move it. "Heavy as iron, too. If it carries away, it will sink like an anchor."

"She'll have a spare." Gillen pointed up at the stern. "See how the rudderpost is rigged? They can haul it up if need be."

A three-bladed brass propeller was mounted forward of the rudder. "That's a small wheel for a boat this size," Larsen said.

"It's just right for the 150-horsepower engine she'll have."

"Why, that's only half the power she'll need!" Larsen's blue eyes widened.

"She's primarily a sailing ship—the engine is auxiliary."

"But this is 1928. The days of sail are over."

"They've got a reason. This ship is the idea of Inspector Wood, who commanded the Western Arctic for some years. He felt the R.C.M.P. needed a small auxiliary schooner with plenty of cruising range. When she was approved, they had only so much money to spend, so they decided they could get the most range by designing her for sail. Big engines are

11

expensive, take up lots of room, and need tons of fuel, but wind is free."

"She'll have cruising range, all right, but it will take forever to get anywhere in the Arctic under canvas. When you're beset in the ice you go where the wind and current take you, but with a powerful enyine you can usually ram your way out."

"We know that," Captain Gillen agreed ruefully. "But government decisions aren't made by sailors."

"They've got a good hull here," Larsen said, "but they might lose it because the politicians chiseled on an enyine. I'll bet most of her cruising will be under power and the sails will be the auxiliary."

"That will be for the skipper to decide. I was hired to deliver her to Herschel Island and that's all."

A heavyset man with a black moustache looked down from the deck above. He wore the working uniform of a constable of the Royal Canadian Mounted Police—billed cap and khaki tunic and trousers. "Hello, Cap! Who's your friend?"

"Come on down, Jack. I'd like to have you meet him. You may be shipmates later on."

The burly Mountie stepped over the bulwark onto the vessel's guard, hopped to the staging, and descended agilely for a man of his size. He was about Larsen's height, five-feet-ten, but was thirty or so pounds heavier than Larsen's solid 175. Gillen introduced them. "Jack, this is Henry Larsen, the ice pilot you've heard Corporal Pasley speak about. Captain Larsen, meet the vessel's chief engineer, Constable Jack Foster. He and Pasley are keeping an eye on construction for the R.C.M.P." They shook hands.

"Pasley says you've a real nose for ice," Foster said.

Larsen grinned. "Where is Ernie?"

"He'll be down soon." The constable had a warm manner. A sparkle in his eyes betrayed a sense of humor and a zest for living. Larsen felt he'd known him all his life. They were of about the same age—twenty-eight.

"Have you got much time in enyine rooms, Yack?"

"I've never been to sea except as a passenger."

"How come they made you chief enyineer?"

"I've worked with motors most of my life. I was in the Royal Canadian Flying Corps during the war. When I got this assignment I was attached to the motor section at the Vancouver Police Barracks."

"Running a marine diesel is different from tinkering with cars."

"Well, Henry, the R.C.M.P. doesn't give you a job unless they think you can handle it. And then you'd better!"

This man would do, Larsen thought. He had the look of a dependable shipmate.

Captain Gillen looked at his watch. "I've got to get back to town, Jack. Would you show Larsen the rest of the ship?"

"I'll take care of him, Cap." When Gillen had gone, Foster said, "What do you think of her?"

"You can't tell much about a ship till she's been to sea, but she looks pretty good except for that wheel." He indicated the propeller. "It's way too small. She's going to be underpowered for what she has to do. And that's not the hull of a sailing ship. It's too round, and the keel isn't deep enough to grip the sea. She won't sail into the wind at all, but she'll be fine in the ice."

"That's what Ernie Pasley keeps saying."

"Do you know how tall her sticks will be?"

"The mainmast will be sixty-five feet and the foremast a little less."

"Too tall. When she rolls she won't want to come back unless she's loaded to her scuppers." Larsen shook his head.

"I'll take your word for it. Let's go topside."

They climbed the staging to the stern and looked around. The workmanship was flawless, and Larsen commented on it.

13

"Most of the people working on her are old-country moss-backs," Foster said. "They may not get another chance to build a wooden ship, so they're putting their best into her."

"When is she to be launched?"

"Early in May. They tell me we have to sail before the end of June to get around Point Barrow before the fall ice moves in."

The decks were laid but not yet caulked. Through the open seams they could see lights burning below and hear the voices of the shipwrights, the tapping of their hammers, and the singing of their saws.

They descended a ladder to the engine room. There was no machinery in it, only the end of the propeller shaft protruding from the stuffing box. "What do you think of the size of those ribs?"

"Real skookum!" Henry Larsen had to shout to be heard above the pounding of the caulkers' mallets.

They looked aft through a doorway into an area bulkheaded into several small compartments. "That cubbyhole over there on the starboard side is the wireless room, and the one to port will be the galley." They went through another doorway farther aft and into an area where shipwrights were installing bunks and lockers. "This is the saloon and after cabin." There were several portholes on either side.

"Who will bunk in here?" Larsen asked.

"The second engineer, cook, wireless operator, and myself."

"Where will the captain and navigator be?"

"In a cabin in the deckhouse. The mate and deckhands will be in the fo'c's'le forward. She's supposed to carry a crew of nine but has accommodations for fourteen."

"She's nice and roomy," the Norwegian commented.

"We may be cooped up in here for years at a time, so we might as well be comfortable."

They returned topside and walked up the well deck.

Foster looked down the companionway forward of the well deck. "Too many down there now. We'd just be in the way. I suppose you've seen plenty of fo'c's'les."

"I sailed first when I was twelve years old," Larsen assured him.

"There's eight bunks down there, a bit more crowded than aft."

"Who designed her?"

"The specifications were prepared by the naval constructor of the Department of Marine in Ottawa, but when the builder saw the original design he wouldn't touch it. Said he wouldn't endanger his reputation by building such a craft unless modifications were made to the plans. They were, and here she sits."

"Has she got a name yet?"

"Right now she's Wallace Hull No. 114. The Minister of Justice has been asked to name her. It isn't official yet, but I hear he's picked the name of a parish in his constituency of Quebec East."

"Have you heard what it is?"

"*St. Roch.*"

"*Saint Rock,*" repeated the Norwegian, trying the name on his tongue.

[2]

"HEY, JACK! Are you aboard?" The words, coming up from overside, were bellowed loud enough to be heard above the sound of shipyard noises and wind and flapping canvas roofing.

Foster looked over the bulwark. "We're up on the bow, Ernie!"

"Did Henry Larsen show up?"

"He's right here!"

Larsen looked down at the stocky Mounted Policeman wearing two yellow chevrons on his sleeve. "Hello, Ernie!"

"Hello, Henry! Did you get a good look at her?"

"Everything worth seeing."

"Let's go up to the office and have a mug-up."

Foster and Larsen went over the side and down the scaffolding to the ways. Corporal Pasley shook hands with Henry. "Long time no see. What's it been—three years, four?"

"You were at Baillie Island when we stopped there on our way to Wilmot Island in the *Old Maid.*"

"That would be '24. When did you leave Klingenberg?"

"I came out in '25."

"Have you been at Prince Rupert ever since?"

"Yah, I bought a salmon boat and been fishing up there. I sold it when I got your letter. I was already fed up with

16

that fishing game. Besides, it rains too much up there, and I was getting homesick for the Arctic, too. Say, how did you know I was at Prince Rupert?"

"Any place Henry Larsen is, everybody knows it."

"Especially the Mounted Police, eh?"

"Maybe we'd better check his fingerprints before he gets away," Jack Foster said.

"We can do that later. Let's go have that coffee."

When they were sitting around a table in the shipyard office, Henry put sugar and cream in his coffee and stirred it. "So I have to yoin the Mounted Police to get this yob of navigator, eh?"

Pasley nodded. "Are you a Canadian citizen yet?"

"No."

"How long have you been in Canada altogether?"

"Besides the time I've been at Prince Rupert, I was sailing in Canadian waters with Klinky for over two years."

"You have plenty of time in, then. You should have no trouble getting citizenship."

"For how long do I have to yoin the R.C.M.P.?"

"Three years or five."

"Three years can be a long time. What if I don't like it?"

"You can buy out. But if you stay for thirty you get a pension."

"Maybe I should start thinking about my old age."

"The R.C.M.P. isn't an old folk's home, I promise you that."

"It would be a good chance to get back to the Arctic."

"We don't have much time left. Why don't you give me some personal information to show the superintendent?" Pasley opened a notebook. "When and where were you born?"

"September 30, 1899, at Fredrikstad, Norway, the next town to Sarpsborg, where Roald Amundsen comes from."

"You were in the Norwegian Navy, weren't you?"

"Yah, but only for six months. Then I went to the Poly-

17

technic of Navigation and studied for officer's papers. After that I was on transatlantic motor ships for a time. I got to be a first officer."

"You hold a master's ticket, don't you?"

"Yah."

"Are you married?"

"No. I'm married to the sea."

"I guess that's all I need to know now. Is there anything you want to do, Henry?"

"You better take me where I've got to go to see about yoining the Mounted Police."

Royal Canadian Mounted Police officials at the Vancouver Barracks made the necessary arrangements for Henry Asbjorn Larsen to become a citizen of the Dominion of Canada. Then he was examined, found fit to meet the standards of the R.C.M.P., swore allegiance to the king, and took the oath of office of a Mounted Policeman. He was given Regimental Number 10407 and assigned to duty as a crew member of the floating detachment vessel being built at North Vancouver. The technicalities over, Corporal Pasley shook his hand. "You're one of us now, Constable."

In addition to work clothing and the regulation khaki uniform, Larsen was issued the distinctive dress uniform of the Mounted Police. He tried on the blue riding trousers with wide yellow stripes down the outer seam and the gold-buttoned scarlet tunic with blue shoulder straps and throat tabs and silver badges on the collar. He put on the leather Sam Browne belt with its strap running diagonally across his chest and over the left shoulder. Pulling on high-topped boots and donning the broad-brimmed Stetson hat, he looked in the mirror. "By golly, now I *look* like a Mountie, too!" he said to Foster, who was watching.

"Not yet, Henry," Foster said. "You don't have your spurs on." He put the blunt spurs in place above Larsen's boot

18

heels and fastened the buckles. *"Now* you look like a Mountie."

"That ship will be a rough one to ride, but I didn't think I'd need spurs."

"Take a good look at yourself then put that outfit in the bottom of your seabag, Henry," Pasley said. "When we leave here you won't wear it for a long, long time."

He examined the Force's badge. A wreath of maple leaves surrounded the motto *"Maintiens le Droit,"* which in turn encircled a buffalo head. Above was a jeweled crown and "Canada." At the bottom of the badge was a banner with "Royal Canadian Mounted Police" on it. He asked the meaning of *"Maintiens le Droit."*

"Maintain the right."

"Do you suppose I could go riding while I'm here? I love horses."

"I wouldn't bank on it, Henry. You have some busy days ahead."

They *were* busy days. R.C.M.P. recruits were usually sent to "Depot" Division at Regina, Saskatchewan, for training. Because time was so short, Henry Larsen was given the basic instructions at the Police Barracks. Sea legs rebelled at foot drill, but he enjoyed the shooting. Although he did well with the .303 rifle, it took some practice to qualify with the .45 caliber revolver. Courses in law enforcement and R.C.M.P. regulations were difficult because the English terms were unfamiliar. In turn, some instructors found his Norwegian accent hard to understand. But he was a willing student, and they had patience with him.

In a lecture on the history and traditions of the Force, Larsen heard how, in 1873, the first Prime Minister of Canada, Sir John A. Macdonald, had drafted a parliamentary bill to raise six troops of cavalry, three hundred men, to control the lawless prairies of mid-continent. He called them "Mounted Rifles" and outfitted them in crimson coats,

19

patterned after the uniform of the colonial British army, the insignia of men who had never broken faith with an Indian tribe. When United States newspapers headlined that Canada was raising an expeditionary force that might endanger U.S. interests in the West, Sir John changed the word "Rifles" to "Police."

The new recruit learned how George French, a Royal Artillery colonel, officer commanding the Canadian School of Gunnery, drilled his recruits from dawn to dusk at the stonewalled frontier post, Fort Garry. Then he marched them eight hundred miles to the Rockies to take Fort Whoop-up, a stronghold of outlaws in the heart of the Blackfoot nation. Under the leadership of Assistant Commissioner James Macleod, a hard-drinking, black-bearded Scot, they eliminated the whiskey traders without firing a shot and forever won the gratitude of the Indian chiefs.

Another legendary figure that impressed Henry Larsen was J. M. Walsh, commandant of Fort Walsh. In the company of a sergeant, three constables, and a scout, he rode boldly into the camp of Sitting Bull and two thousand Sioux warriors after they had wiped out Custer and his men and escaped to Canada. Walsh faced the chief and told him that if they were to stay they must obey the laws of Canada. Sitting Bull and his subchiefs assented. The Mounted Policemen spent the night in a tepee of the Sioux, and in the morning arrested an Assiniboin horse thief who rode into the camp on a stolen mount.

Larsen heard about other men, famous within the Force, such as Charles Constantine who'd established police control in the Klondike in 1894. In 1903 he'd founded the first detachment in the Western Arctic. Under his direction, Mounties built a six hundred-mile trail up the Peace River from Alberta to the Klondike.

This was the old North West Mounted Police, Larsen learned. Because of their deeds they were honored by King

Edward VII in 1904 when he conferred the prefix "Royal" on their name.

The lecturer spoke of the World War I record of Mounted Policemen who had gone to France as Squadron "D" of the Canadian Light Horse. Hurried home at war's end, they put down a bloody general strike in Winnipeg, earning the hatred of seditious communists. To forestall future troubles, the Royal North West Mounted Police was combined with the Dominion Police in February of 1920 to become a national force, the Royal Canadian Mounted Police.

"A lot of good men gave their lives to make this Force what it is," said the speaker pointedly.

One day when Larsen's period of instruction was almost finished, an orderly came looking for him. "The OC wants to see you."

He presented himself to Assistant Commissioner Duffus, commander of the barracks. "How are you getting along, Larsen?"

"Yust fine, sir."

"Is there anything we can do for you, anything you need?"

"Well, sir, I wonder if I could go over to the stables and ride one of those horses?"

"Larsen, you're a sailor. Stay away from the stables. One of those remounts is liable to kick your head off and you've got a mighty important job ahead of you."

[3]

SPRING CAME to southern British Columbia. The chill winds of winter that blew off the Coast Mountains and pelted rain into the building shed changed to warm winds pelting rain into the building shed. Regardless of the weather, Constable Larsen was usually there.

Recruit training finished, he continued to live at the Barracks, coming by ferry each day to the shipyard with Corporal Pasley and Jack Foster. They would review the plans and work schedule, then go to the vessel and examine what had been done the day before.

Captain Gillen was around a lot too. "I wish I were twenty years younger, Larsen. I'd be tempted to join the Force to have your job."

"You'd have to fight for it, Cap."

The hull caulking was finished, the seams packed with putty, the hull painted with red lead and covered with strips of black Irish felt. Then the steam-softened ironbark, tough Australian gumwood, was sheathed on. Steel plates were bolted to the bow, a waterline was drawn, and everything below it was covered with several coats of red preservative. Above the waterline she was painted gray with a band of white along the bulwarks.

During April most of the interior work was completed.

The fir masts, booms, and gaffs were brought to the wood-working shed, and layers of spar varnish applied. As the completion deadline neared, Wallace Hull No. 114 swarmed with workmen—painters, shipwrights, electricians, and riggers.

The rest of the crew were arriving at the Barracks. A. F. C. Tudor was to be mate and M. J. Olsen, Alcide Lamothe, and T. J. Parsloe, deckhands. A civilian, Special Constable Seeley, was hired as wireless operator. The second engineer, R. W. Kells, was already in the Arctic and would join at Herschel Island.

The cook was William J. Parry, a man older than any of them. Upon meeting him, Larsen said, "You have the most important job on the ship." They became close friends, though at times each had difficulty understanding the other's accent—Parry was a Welshman. A graying man in his mid-forties who had worked on North Sea trawlers as a boy, he had joined the old Royal North West Mounted Police in 1919, the same year as Jack Foster. He had a reputation in the Force for being an all-around handyman, willing to do any job assigned. Everybody called him "Dad."

One day in early May, a few days before the launching, Pasley took a call in the office. Hanging up, he said, "The name is official now." "ST. ROCH" was lettered in black on either side of the bow and on the stern, with "OTTAWA" below. A worker grumbled, "It should be 'Vancouver.' This will be her home port."

"The main thing is we've got our ship," the corporal said. "I don't care if she's got 'Timbuktu' on her."

" 'Rock' sounds safer," answered another worker.

The decks were caulked, and when the oakum was in the seams the cracks were filled with hot pitch. In the sail loft, canvas was taking shape under horny hands.

As launching day approached, chips and shavings, lumber ends and sawdust were cleaned up and carted off. The scaffolding was knocked apart and taken away. The schooner stood clean and fresh in glistening paintwork, stern toward the harbor.

At low tide in the early afternoon of May 7, shipyard men in rubber boots, with mops and pails of melted tallow, greased the ways. The heavy chains that held the cradle to the land were unshackled. Only wedges kept the ship from sliding down the incline.

The evening ceremonies were simple. At high tide the wife of Superintendent Newsome, officer commanding "E" Division, Vancouver, said, "I christen thee *St. Roch!*" and smashed a bottle of champagne against the bow. Workmen knocked the wedges free, and the ship started sliding toward the water. The head rigger turned to Foster. "Take a good look, Jack. That's the fastest trip she'll ever make."

The *St. Roch* hit the water with a splash, floated free of the cradle, and was snubbed to a pier by mooring lines.

While she lay there for two days "soaking up," the fuel and water tanks, auxiliary engines, and bilge pumps were installed. On the morning of the third day she was moved into position where a derrick hoisted the main engine and lowered it into the engine room. The vessel settled a few inches by the stern. Foster, Pat Kelly, the factory engineer, and the marine mechanics connected shafts and gears, fuel lines and controls, and prepared the engine for running.

The deckhouse was lifted aboard and bolted into place above the engine room. The derrick then set the anchor windlass on the forecastle head for fastening. Anchor chains were fed through pipes down into the forepeak, rove through rings at the bottom of the chain locker, and secured. The anchors were attached and fetched up snug. On the well deck, a cargo winch was installed.

With each additional piece of equipment the *St. Roch* sank a trifle deeper in the water. But she still floated high and rocked in the wake of each passing craft. "We're going to have to ballast her before we put the sticks in," Larsen warned, "or she might roll over here at the dock."

The fuel and water tanks were filled, but when the masts were stepped and rigged she was still cranky. "I won't move her until we get another fifty tons in her," Captain Gillen said.

They stowed 110 drums of diesel oil in the hold, and Larsen made a calculation. "That's only twenty tons."

"We'll start loading coal, then," Pasley said, They floored off the barrel tops with lumber and stowed thirty tons of coal.

"That's more like it," Gillen said. "She's safe now."

Parry began bringing stores aboard. Deckhands filled the coal bin, and a fire was lighted in the galley stove. Soon smoke and the scent of coffee began to permeate the vessel. Sniffing, Larsen said, "She's a real ship now." Going below, he had his first cup of coffee aboard the *St. Roch*.

The engine was started. Its tremors vibrated through the vessel. She seemed to come to life. The gears were tested, and with the turning of the propeller first one way, then the other, the ship surged forward and aft against the lines that held her.

Pilothouse equipment was installed—the steering wheel, a compass, the telegraph for transmitting orders to the engine room, a speaking tube for voice communication, a barometer and chronometer. "Nothing fancy," Larsen said, "but we've got what we need to navigate."

A wooden rifle rack was put on the right-hand bulkhead. In the chart room and stateroom at the rear of the deckhouse were a barometer, repeater compass, and chronometer, and bunks for the captain and navigator. The interior was finished in dark walnut paneling. "You'd almost think she was a yacht," Pasley said.

A motor launch and a whaleboat were slung from davits on each side of the afterdeck.

The sails were brought aboard and bent to booms, gaffs,

and mast hoops. As the stiff new canvas was hoisted for the first time, Captain Gillen said, "The jib and fores'l look all right, but what's your opinion of that mains'l, Henry?"

"You can't really tell till we get her out in a good breeze, but yust looking I'd say it's way too big for the ship."

"That's what I was thinking."

"Pat Kelly says the enyine room is ready. I'll talk to them at the office and see if we can take her out tomorrow on a shakedown cruise."

Foster went to the office with him. He came back alone. "We're taking her out right after breakfast in the morning.

"Did you call Pasley at the barracks and tell him?"

"He won't be coming with us, Henry. He had a disagreement with the superintendent about procedure. Said if he couldn't run the *St. Roch* his own way, they'd better get a new skipper. Newsome said that would be just fine, so Ernie's out."

Larsen shook his head. "That's too bad. I was afraid he was heading for trouble. I wonder who will take his place?"

"Unless somebody says otherwise, I guess you will."

A meeting of the crew was held that evening at the barracks. The superintendent presided. "You all know that while Corporal Pasley was considered to be captain of the *St. Roch,* technically he was first mate. His appointment as skipper was not to have been effective until the vessel reached Herschel Island. Captain Gillen is master until Inspector Kemp accepts the ship. Is that clearly understood?"

Everyone nodded.

"Because of seniority policies, I am appointing Constable Tudor first mate and Olsen second mate. Larsen will be navigator."

Constable Tudor stood up. "Might I make a point, sir?"

"Certainly."

"I don't feel seniority should apply, sir. What counts at

sea is experience. Constable Larsen has more sea time than the rest of us put together. He's the man for the first mate's job."

"That's generous of you. Olsen, what are your feelings?"

"Larsen is the man, sir."

"Does anybody object to taking orders from a recruit?"

"No, sir."

"Not at all!"

"All right, Larsen, the job is yours. Good luck."

"Thank you, sir."

"Tudor will be second mate and Olsen a deckhand. All assignments are only temporary for the voyage to Herschel. Inspector Kemp will make permanent appointments up there."

Captain Gillen came aboard the *St. Roch* shortly after eight in the morning. The engine was idling, and everybody was in the saloon having coffee. Besides the crew, several shipyard specialists were there. The captain sat down and Parry set a mug of steaming coffee before him.

"Where are we going today, Cap?" Larsen asked.

"We'll go out and run the measured mile off Kitsilano Beach a few times. I wanted to try the sails, but there's no wind today."

They had hoped to get an early start, but they had to wait for some of the local R.C.M.P. officers who were coming along with their wives. When all were aboard Gillen said, "Let's get out of here."

Pat Kelly, Foster, and the mechanical specialists went to the engine room. Gillen and Larsen, the rest of the crew, and guests went topside. At a signal from Gillen the small yard tug moored ahead cast off and chugged away.

"Cast off fore and aft!"

The mooring lines were thrown off the bollards by dockmen, hauled aboard, and coiled. The vessel began drifting away from the pier, borne by the ebbing tide. Gillen pushed the pointer of the telegraph to "Slow Ahead." A gong jangled below, and the sound of the engine deepened. Water roiled astern, a ripple spread away from the bow, and the *St. Roch* moved under her own power for the first time.

Henry Larsen looked at the clock, and in a fresh new logbook wrote at the top of the first page the date and the words, "Cruising off Vancouver, B.C." On the line below he entered the time and, "Under way on shakedown cruise."

Captain Gillen was at the helm. Beyond the pier he pointed the bow westward down Burrard Inlet toward the First Narrows. The accompanying tug trailed along off the port quarter. Outside the Narrows, the *St. Roch* began to lift and dip to a glassy swell rolling in from the Strait of Georgia. Gillen turned the helm over to Larsen. "Take her into English Bay and we'll make a couple of runs to see if she will do her eight knots."

Henry turned the vessel south and moved the telegraph to "Full Ahead." The gong clanged, the beat of the engine quickened. White water washed away from the bow and boiled out astern. They crossed English Bay, and half a mile off Kitsilano Beach turned westward. The shore marker at the beginning of the measured mile came abeam. Captain Gillen noted the time. When they passed the second marker he said: "Eight minutes—seven and a half knots. Put her about and we'll make a run the other way."

The second run over the course was made in a fraction over seven minutes. "There's a little easterly current in here," the captain said. "Eight and a half knots plus seven and a half is sixteen. Divide that by two and we've got the eight knots the contract calls for."

They made another run over the measured mile, then continued on to the west, leaving a wake that broke against the sea walls and washed up on the bathing beaches skirting the southern section of Vancouver. When they reached Point Grey, Gillen said, "Take her back to the yard, Henry."

Larsen brought the vessel about on a course that would take her back to the Narrows, then turned the helm over to Olsen. Going out on deck, he watched the bubbling wake flowing out clean and straight astern, the sign of a good man at the wheel. Henry listened to the ship sounds and heard a creaking that should not be there. Up forward he found a foremast stay was slack. In tightening it he noted that the backstays hadn't been installed yet.

A gull settled atop the mainmast for a ride. They passed swimming ducks, a drifting log with cormorants on it, a snakelike kelp, and a dead and smelly fish. Larsen savored the sea with all his senses. He saw it around him, felt it lift the vessel, smelled it in the air, tasted its salt, and heard it rippling by. He felt sorry for landsmen.

On several more shakedown cruises, minor defects were found and corrected. The *St. Roch* was officially completed on June 19. The backstays still hadn't been installed, but that could be done going up the Inside Passage. The sails were hoisted a time or two, but no wind blew strong enough to give her a trial under canvas. Her sailing ability could be well tested on the way to Herschel Island.

Summer began warm and bright. The younger crew members were anxious to be off to the North. "Be patient, lads," Dad Parry said. "There'll be a lot of waiting in the Arctic."

The following week the ship was moved to Vancouver and moored at the Evans, Coleman, and Evans dock for final loading. A Hudson's Bay Company ship, the *Baychimo* of Liverpool, was in port, taking on cargo for the firm's Arctic trading posts. In other years she had carried R.C.M.P. freight too, but this time the *St. Roch* would carry it.

Stevedores filled the hold with crates and boxes, barrels of ship's stores and supplies for the detachments, cases of ammunition, and cans of black gunpowder. Over the crammed full hold, the hatch covers were put on and tarpaulins battened down. A hundred more drums of diesel oil were stowed on the well deck and sacked coal put wherever there was room. Lashed down piles of lumber completed the deck cargo.

The fantail was loaded with cased tins of kerosine and gasoline. Spare machinery parts were stored in the engine room. Galley bins and lockers were filled with food. When fuel and water tanks had been topped off, a spectator said, "She looks like a submarine about to go under."

The crew drew kit and moved their belongings from the barracks to the vessel. The eight Mounties had been issued navy-blue jerseys with "R.C.M.P." on them. An instrument man came aboard, and a two-hour cruise was made around the harbor to adjust the compasses. Then, on the afternoon of June 25, Captain Gillen announced, "We're sailing at high tide tomorrow afternoon."

[4]

AFTERNOON HIGH WATER at Vancouver on June 26, 1928, was at 2:04 P.M. By eight in the morning the crew was aboard, the last few straggling wearily down the gangplank long after daybreak following "one last night on the town." Captain Gillen was last to arrive. Smelling strongly of spirits, he had to be helped from a taxicab to his bunk by the driver and Jack Foster.

As first mate, Henry Larsen was in charge of the vessel. When all had breakfasted and changed to work clothes, he turned them to, tightening lashings and securing cargo. He was unsympathetic to complaints of headaches and sleepiness. "Work up a sweat and you'll be all right."

It wasn't hard to sweat. A hot sun had risen before four and was reflected from the water. Except for a few clouds in the south, the sky was clear. There was no wind, but predictions were "Westerlies later in the day and possible showers tomorrow."

At ten Larsen knocked the crew off. "Get cleaned up and put on those new sweaters. We're going to have our pictures taken."

By eleven, families, friends, well-wishers, and the curious were roaming the vessel. Newspapermen arrived at noon, and the officials came at one o'clock. The captain, rested and spruced up, met them at the head of the gangplank. There was no formal leave-taking ceremony, only wishing of good luck and a prosperous voyage. Reporters from the Vancouver *Sun* and *Province* interviewed the crew, and photographers took their pictures. At a quarter of two Captain Gillen said, "I'm afraid everyone will have to leave now. We want to go out of the Narrows on the first of the ebb tide."

There was much shaking of hands and many farewell kisses as the visitors left the ship. The gangway was brought aboard, lines cast off, the whistle blew, and the *St. Roch* backed away from the dock. Henry Larsen made an entry in the log: "2:00 p.m. Under way from Vancouver to Arctic Ocean."

The tide was ebbing well when they passed through the First Narrows and steamed westward. Two hours later the course was changed to northwest. The first leg of the voyage would be by way of the Inside Passage, 250 miles of sheltered but treacherous currents.

Sea watches had been set at noon. Larsen was in charge of the twelve-to-four, and Olsen was his seaman. At four P.M. Larsen made a round of the vessel to see that everything was secure. Satisfied, he turned the watch over to Captain Gillen and went below for coffee.

He stopped by the wireless room where Seeley was fiddling with the Marconi set. "Anything new about Captain Amundsen, Sparks?"

"The afternoon news is just coming on. I'll try to get it."

While they waited for the news broadcast, Larsen thought of events on the other side of the earth. On May 25, Umberto Nobile, Italian explorer and aviator, had crashed north of Siberia while returning from a flight over the Pole in the dirigible *Italia*. Half a dozen expeditions had been organized to try to save the survivors. Nobile was rescued by a Russian flyer.

On June 19, just a week ago, Roald Amundsen and five

others had taken off in a French Navy seaplane from Tromso, Norway, to hunt for the missing crew of the airship. They had not been heard from.

The news announcer had nothing new to report. "Roald Amundsen and his companions are presumed to be lost."

Seeley switched off the set. "Do you think they're alive?"

"If they were in a boat or afoot on the ice, Amundsen would bring them through." Larsen shook his head. "But too many things could happen in an airplane that he had no control over."

He went to the stateroom in the deckhouse and turned in. It had been a long day and he was tired, but sleep was slow in coming. When he was a boy, the explorer had been his hero, when a young man, his inspiration. One did not easily give up hope for a man of Amundsen's stature. He had turned up before after years-long absences in both Arctic and Antarctic.

In the summer of 1903 Amundsen and his crew had entered the Arctic by way of Baffin Bay in an old fishing sloop, the forty-seven-ton *Gjoa*. The objective was to try to be the first to go from the Atlantic to the Pacific over the top of the North American continent by way of the Northwest Passage. After being out of contact with the outside world for three years, they had reached San Francisco in August of 1906. The *St. Roch* was heading into the same waters.

Larsen had often wondered what drove the hawk-faced Amundsen and other explorers to do the things they did. Was it a simple desire to be the first to do what no one else had done, or was it hunger for publicity and personal glory? Explorer, businessman, or politician, it was the egotistical person who drove himself to success rather than face the disgrace of failure. Whatever his motives, Amundsen was no phony.

Henry Larsen had his own lifelong dreams. He had admired his famous countryman, and envied him as well. But what could a man do now to equal the deeds of Amundsen and the other great navigators of the past? What was left to be accomplished? Henry Larsen could think of only two things that remained: to sail from west to east through the Northwest Passage, and to circumnavigate the North American continent. He knew his destiny was in the Arctic. That's why he was going back.

Everything northbound passed the *St. Roch* except two men rowing in a dory. She cruised slowly by floating logging camps, bunkhouses on rafts moored to shore. Pairs of husky loggers felled timber on slopes so steep the toppled trees slid all the way to the water. Indians in dugout canoes fished with nets at creek mouths or jigged for bottom fish in the kelp beds on the reefs. The *St. Roch* passed their ramshackle villages where weathered totem poles stood like specters in the shadows of the forest.

"This is Haida country," Olsen said. "In the old days we'd have lost our heads here."

Expecting to reach the ocean on the evening of June 28, the master ordered all work done before the ship left quiet waters. Parry spent the day baking bread and pastries and frying doughnuts for days ahead. The off-watch mates and deckhands tightened lashings and pumped diesel oil from drums on deck to the main tanks to replace consumed fuel. The engineers cleaned the oil strainers, and when they docked at an Alert Bay cannery to top off fuel and water tanks, the engine, clutch, and gears were checked.

When she got under way again the *St. Roch* was ready for the sea. The sun was setting north of northwest and the horizon was afire as she left Johnstone Strait at eight o'clock. Two hours later the vessel passed the winking lighthouse on Scarlet Point and lifted to the Pacific swell. Captain Gillen came from the stateroom. "Queen Charlotte Sound, eh?"

"Time to change course, Captain?" Tudor asked.

34

"No, we'll go up Hecate Strait and head west from Dixon Entrance."

A heavy swell was rolling in from sea and soon most of the landlubbers were seasick. For twenty-four hours the ship wallowed and pitched before reaching shelter in Hecate Strait, east of the Queen Charlotte Islands. Thirty more hours brought the *St. Roch* to Dixon Entrance, and another half day's steaming, to the Pacific. A westward course was set for Dutch Harbor. Soon the scent of shore and forested islands was gone. Only the smell of ship and sea remained.

The wind and swell were out of the west and almost every sea broke over the vessel's stubby nose. Forecastlehead and deck load were drenched. Salt from the blowing spray blinded the windows of the pilothouse.

Just before four o'clock the morning after leaving Dixon Entrance, Larsen took the wheel so Olsen could go forward and awaken Lamothe to go on watch. He saw the man hesitate, look over the side, then hurry back. "We're sinking, Henry! There's a foot of water in the well deck and the bulwarks are nearly awash!"

Larsen blew the whistle on the voice tube. Pat Kelly answered. "What'll you have up there?"

"Is there any water in the bilge?"

"She's dry as a bone."

"Take the wheel, Ole." Henry hurried to the hand pump forward of the house. He worked the handle, but it sucked dry. There was no water in the hold. He made his way over the deck load and down the companionway into the forecastle. He listened for water sloshing in the bilge, but heard none. Awakening Lamothe, Larsen returned topside. There certainly was a foot of water washing around on the well deck. The bulwarks were completely awash at times, and the scuppers were submerged. He returned to the pilothouse, grinning.

"What's funny?" Olsen asked.

"The water breaking aboard has soaked into the lumber and coal on deck. No wonder she's down over her marks."

"Do you think she'll settle much more?"

"A little, maybe. But there's enough buoyancy in the living spaces and enyine room to keep us afloat even if she goes down another foot. If our hatches don't get stove in and no one leaves a porthole open, we'll stay on top."

"I sure hope so."

The second day away from land the wind shifted to the southeast and the sails were hoisted. The heavily loaded vessel gained little speed from the taut canvas but rode steadier under it.

Crossing the Gulf of Alaska they saw nothing but an occasional halibut boat tending its lines and the distant wisp of a steamer's smoke. The only sign of man they saw was his rubbish. Even on the vastest of oceans it was plentiful—drifting tins and bottles, cantaloupe and grapefruit rinds, and empty boxes.

The following gulls had deserted. But brown gooneys, the sooty albatross, soared endlessly on unmoving wings, skimming close to wave tops. Shy puffins, with comical, gaudy beaks like parrots paddled away when the ship came near. Friendly dolphins, black with white bellies, darted alongside and underneath the bow. Not so friendly were the sinister dorsals that occasionally cut the wake astern. Their ominous presence ensured the use of the lifelines strung about the vessel. *St. Roch* passed through a great shoal of herring and whales, glistening brutes as big as the ship, which blew a smelly steam as they surfaced to breathe and feed on the herring.

Those who hadn't yet found their sea legs were prone to stay in their bunks with their misery, but Larsen put them to work on deck. "Fresh air is what you need, not a stinking fo'c'sle."

After a few days the crew felt that there was only one

world—the world of the vessel and the surrounding ocean. Memories of the past were distant. "It seems as though we've never done anything but sail and sail and sail."

"It's like waiting for the breakup in the Arctic," Larsen said. "You get the feeling it's always been winter and always will be."

The twice-daily wireless schedules kept them in touch with reality. Amundsen and the missing airmen had not yet been found.

Someone was always going aft to check the mileage on the taffrail log, the torpedo-shaped rotator trailing astern at the end of a line. Sextant observations pinpointed where they were.

The master was satisfied with their progress. On the eighth day after leaving Vancouver, a noon observation of the sun showed the *St. Roch* to be five hundred miles south of Cape St. Elias and more than a third of the way across the Gulf of Alaska. The chart indicated a depth of 2,137 fathoms.

"We're only two and a half miles from land—straight down."

The sky was blue, the sun was bright, and the deckhands worked bare-chested.

"Enjoy it while you can, boys," the captain said.

That night during Larsen's watch the barometer dropped abruptly. The wind died, and clouds began to obscure the northern stars. Henry roused Gillen. "Looks like a norther coming, Cap."

The off-watch men were awakened, jib and foresail were lowered, and the mainsail reefed. A sea anchor was broken out, lashings were checked and tightened. They were ready when the gale struck.

It came abruptly and directly out of the north. Bitter cold and violent, it proved true all that had been said about *St. Roch* not being a sea boat. She *was* seaworthy or she wouldn't have stayed afloat under the pounding of the norther. But her round hull and little keel were liabilities in a Force 10 blow before winds of fifty-five knots and more.

She yawed and wallowed and pitched, but she was at her worst when she rolled. She would go far over and hang there as though she would never come back to an even keel. But she always straightened up, only to roll the other way with a snap.

"It's that blasted mainmast!" Gillen swore. "I knew it was too tall!"

With the onset of the blow, seasickness returned. Of the deck force only Gillen, Larsen, Tudor, and Olsen were able to stand watches. They did six hours on and six off, with Seeley, a seasoned seaman, taking an occasional turn at the wheel. Little was seen of the engineers. The bells were answered promptly, but their voices, coming through the speaking tube, sounded miserable and weary.

Dad Parry wasn't much of a sailor and admitted it, but he managed to keep coffee on the bobbing stove and tried to serve one hot meal a day to those with a will to eat. Once, when Larsen went below for a mug-up, he found the cook hanging on to the water pump, retching. A garbage pail had upset on the galley deck and the atmosphere was dense with eye-stinging smoke from a tipped-over pot of stew scorching on the stove top. Lumps of coal were rolling around underfoot. A gust of wind blew down the chimney, and the stove backfired. The firebox door flew open, scattering hot coals and ashes.

Henry stamped out the sparks. "Having trouble, Dad?"

"If I live out this cruise, I'll sell pencils on the streets of Edmonton before I set foot on a boat again."

The mate kicked the door shut and scraped the burning stew off the stove. "When the sun comes out you'll forget all about it."

It seemed to blow forever, but in two days it ended as

38

abruptly as it had started. The barometer went up, the wind moderated and shifted to the southeast. The banks of low, dark clouds drifted back into the north, revealing sky and sun again. A noon shot showed that the *St. Roch* had drifted fifty miles to the south, but had lost none of her westing. The engine was turned up to half speed and the ship put back on course, quartering into the parade of combing seas still marching out of the north. They subsided in the night, and the engine was increased to full revolutions. The sails were raised in the morning.

Larsen went around opening portholes, skylights, and companionway hatches dogged down at the onset of the blow. The fresh Pacific breeze quickly cleared the foulness from the living quarters. He jerked blankets from the figures huddled in the bunks.

"Hit the deck, boys, your holidays are over! Rise and shine!"

The weather held fine for two days, but as they neared the Aleutians, gales of short duration swept the sea, interspersed by fogs. Then, at dawn of the fifth day after the norther, jagged shadows appeared on the slate-gray ocean ahead. They were identified as the Sanaks, a group of islands south of the tip of the Alaska Peninsula.

"If the weather holds, we'll be in Akutan tonight," Larsen said.

Shortly after noon the Krenitzin Islands appeared. The ship entered a strait and began to meet fog. The islands vanished. Larsen rang the engine down to half speed, then to dead slow. Each minute the whistle was blown and everyone listened for an answer.

Late in the afternoon echoes of the whistle began returning from starboard. "We must be near Akun Island. We should be able to smell our way in pretty soon."

The echoes, bouncing back from cliffs hidden in the fog,

got louder and began returning more quickly. A man went forward to take soundings with the lead line. The repeated splash of the sinker came back through the mist, followed by the call, "No bottom!" Soon the first of the echo was being heard before the last of the toot had left the whistle. The engine was stopped. The vessel drifted. The washing of waves sounded on an unseen shore. "No bottom!"

"No bottom!" mimicked the echo of the leadsman's voice.

At last the interval between whistle and echo began to lengthen.

"We're clear of the point," Larsen said. The engine was started, and they continued on at slow speed. A stench came through the window.

The helmsman grabbed his nose. "Pee-yew! What stinks?"

"The whaling station. Bring her up two points to the north."

He turned the wheel to the right. "We must be almost there."

"We're still a good ten miles away."

They had been navigating by echo up the foggy passage between Akun and Akutan islands for an hour when they heard a deep-toned whistle. Moments later a narrow little steamer with a loaded harpoon gun on her bow took shadowy form close abeam. Rusty and dirty, she was outbound with a bone in her teeth. A blast of greeting from her whistle, a wave from the bearded men in the pilothouse, and the killer boat vanished in the mist astern.

Another blast sounded ahead, and soon they overtook a sister of the killer. She was laboring in from sea with four dead whales in tow, lashed two on each side by heavy chains around the flukes. The *St. Roch* slowed and followed her to Akutan.

A crisp north wind sprang up and cleared the fog as they entered the harbor. Thousands of screeching sea gulls wheeled about the reduction plant and roosted on the roofs of buildings. Inflated whales were moored to buoys offshore. The stench was unbearable. "We won't stay long," the captain promised as they docked.

The whaling station superintendent came aboard. "Sure, you can have all the water you want. Anything else you need?"

"Not a thing."

"How about having supper with us? Nobody ever comes here. We get lonesome."

"We'd like to, but we're short of time."

While the tanks were being filled, most of the crew went for a walk on shore. For the first few steps the ground seemed to be rolling underfoot. They watched a dead whale dragged by steam winch and chains up a ramp. Men in bloody oilskins and rubber boots cut into the carcass with flensing knives. Blubber was peeled off and sent to the try-works for rendering oil. Flesh and skeleton were dissected with power saws and broad axes and reduced to meat and meal.

The whistle of the *St. Roch* called them back. Larsen counted heads. "Where's Dad?"

"He said he was going to the cookhouse. Here he comes now."

Parry was wheeling a big chunk of dark meat down the dock on a hand truck. "What have you got there, Dad?"

"Whale meat for tomorrow's dinner!"

[5]

THEY LEFT THE DOCK and cruised northward into the wind to put the stink of the whaling station behind as soon as possible. Portholes and companionways were opened to speed the airing out of the clinging stench. Rounding a point, the *St. Roch* lifted to the short, steep swell of the Bering Sea.

At eight o'clock Seeley turned on his set and made contact with the United States Army weather station at Point Barrow. The ice was still solid against the coast there. He tapped out the call letters of the steamer *Victoria,* unloading at Nome. Her operator reported that Norton Sound was open, but the U.S. Indian Bureau's *Boxer* had been turned back by floes at Bering Strait.

Captain Gillen conferred with Larsen. "We're eight hundred miles from the strait, Henry. We can make it in a week, but do you think we can get through when we get there?"

"We should get through Bering Strait all right, but unless there is a good south wind we won't get past Lisburne for a while."

"I'd rather lie at Dutch Harbor than in the ice."

"Yah. Maybe we could do some fishing here. We can catch some cod and salt them down when we get to Unalaska."

They hove to for the night. In the morning, lines were

rigged and everyone began fishing over the bulwarks. The hooks were baited with bacon until a cod was caught, then it was cut up for bait. They caught a ton in two hours. "That's plenty, boys. No use catching more than we need." They got under way and cleaned the fish en route. They had boiled cod and potatoes for the noon meal.

Docking at Unalaska village, they bought fresh vegetables, cases of eggs, and sacks of salt at the Alaska Commercial Company. Crossing the bay to Dutch Harbor, they filled the fuel and water tanks and empty oil drums. When they were ready to depart, a southeaster came howling over the treeless mountains to the south.

"This stuff is too dirty to sail in," the captain said.

"Yah, but it should move the ice up north."

Parry roasted the whale meat for supper. The men tasted it cautiously, then ate heartily.

"I'm glad there's plenty left," Foster said. "It'll be good for sandwiches on the night watches."

In the morning the roast was gone. "It tasted like soap when it was cold," Jack said. "I threw it overboard."

The *St. Roch* remained at the Dutch Harbor oil dock for two days waiting for a break in the weather. The crew made adjustments to the engines, salted the codfish, and entertained visitors. Everyone came down to see the Mounties. Most were disappointed that the officers weren't wearing red tunics, Stetsons, and riding boots, but were dressed like any seamen.

On the morning of the third day the wind moderated and shifted to the northwest. Seeley made wireless contact with the *Boxer*. Bering Strait was free of ice.

Captain Gillen ordered the *St. Roch* to sea. Outside Cape Cheerful the sails were hoisted and the ship proceeded north. It rained hard, and the wind was gusty. She pitched and rolled in the choppy Bering Sea. There was more seasickness.

Dark came a little later that day than the night before, and the following daybreak was twenty minutes earlier than the preceding dawn.

"Another week and we'll have the midnight sun," remarked Captain Gillen.

On the slow voyage northward they experienced everything in the way of weather—snow, fog, bitter northern gales and balmy zephyrs from the south. They even saw a bit of sun and blue sky now and then. But in general the sea of Vitus Bering lived up to its evil reputation as the breeding place of foul weather for a quarter of the world. They crossed the 60th parallel, two thirds of the way from equator to Pole, on the fourth day out of Dutch Harbor. The sun rose at half past two and set that evening well after nine. It did not get dark at all that night, only dusky.

At noon the following day the ship was ten miles west of St. Lawrence Island, 150 miles off the Alaskan coast. Rain and spindrift whipped up by a southwest wind prevented sight of the island, but the sea carried signs of the more distant mainland. The water was muddied by sediment eroded from the interior of the continent by the summer floods of the Yukon River. Uprooted trees, clumps of bushes, and soggy chunks of muskeg floated by. The set of the current was north, the wind favorable, and good mileage was logged that day.

The next morning the *St. Roch* went by King Island, a sheer rock beaten by heavy surf. Ramshackle stone and driftwood huts, connected by flimsy walks and shaky ladders, shared cliff space with a rookery where seabirds nested. The strange village of the Eskimo cliff dwellers appeared to be uninhabited.

"Those people are ivory carvers," Captain Gillen said. "They sit up there in those shacks all winter and make souvenirs. When the ice goes out, everybody piles into umiaks and goes to Nome for the summer to sell the stuff."

A few hours later the *St. Roch* put in at Teller, on Port Clarence Bay, to pick up dried salmon dog feed. Anchoring off the village, the men could see reindeer grazing on the low hills inland. People came running to the beach, launched an umiak, and paddled out. The eskimo craft had a framework of wood and bone bound together with rawhide thongs and covered with stitched walrus skins.

The broad-beamed craft, called a woman's boat, was nearly half the length of the *St. Roch* and carried at least forty people of all ages. Bright-eyed babies peeped over mothers' shoulders from their parkas. Some of the older women had blue tattoo marks on their seamy faces. The younger men and boys had hair bobbed off at eyebrow level. Friendly black eyes with Mongoloid lids were set in round, dark-skinned faces. The front teeth of the women were shorter than those of the men. The teeth of the oldest women were worn down to the gums. "That's because they chew skins to soften them," Larsen said.

A white trader was in the umiak. "Your dog feed is ready. Climb in and we'll take you ashore."

Leaving one man aboard for an anchor watch, the rest got in and were paddled to the beach. Larsen inspected the split salmon drying in the sun and wind on wooden racks. "Looks good to me."

The trader spoke some native words. Women and children took the oily, rock-hard fish from the racks and carried it to the umiak. A ton and a half was taken to the ship.

Jack Foster had been admiring the knee-high skin boots the natives were wearing. "I'd like to get a pair of those mukluks."

"Come on over to the store and pick them out."

The whole crew wanted fancy mukluks. At the trading post they picked out what they wanted. The boots were beautifully made of reindeer skin and soled with walrus. Larsen sniffed a pair. "You tan them the old way, eh?"

"This stuff was tanned with deer urine. We don't let the natives use their own for our stock."

The turning up and rounding of the heels and toes of the mukluks was done with closely spaced crimpings in the tough walrus hide. "What kind of tool do they do that with?" Foster asked.

"Their teeth."

"Do they chew it before or after it's tanned?"

"Right out of the vat while it's still soft."

"Ugh!"

They paid for the fish and footwear, and Larsen bought a young Siberian Husky bitch from an Eskimo. He named her Olga. When they were about to leave, the village chief asked if they would stay a bit longer. "We want to have a dance for you guys."

"Do you want to stay for the dance, boys?" Gillen asked.

"Sure!"

A big fire of driftwood was built on the beach, and several reindeer carcasses were set to roasting. The dancing started immediately. Old men sat in a circle on the ground, singing in a minor key, and thumped with sticks on drums of walrus hide stretched on wooden hoops. The dancers, younger men, pranced and stamped to the rhythm of the drums, taking turns singing and pantomiming their favorite stories.

Some were of hunting expeditions, others supernatural tales of witches and evil spirits encountered and defeated. One old man told in song, interpreted by the trader, of a great battle here a century ago, when his father helped defeat invading Chukchi from Siberia. Women's and children's dances followed. Then the Eskimos bounced each other and the Mounties high into the air from a walrus hide ringed by everyone who could find a handhold.

The roasted reindeer meat was carved, dipped in seal oil, and eaten with the fingers. While they feasted, one of the

Mounties noticed people going about their business in the village, apparently ignoring the festivities. The trader explained. "We have a sad situation here—the village is divided. When Amundsen and Nobile flew over the Pole in the *Norge* two years ago, they landed here. Hard feelings had come between them, and they weren't on speaking terms."

The bitterness between the two explorers was common knowledge.

"The Norwegians dealt at my post, and the Italians traded at the other one. My customers sided in with Amundsen, and the ones who dealt at the other store took up Nobile's side of the argument. Half the people still aren't speaking to the others."

"Too bad they got involved," Gillen said. "It's the silliest thing I ever heard of."

"No sillier than two famous men acting like a couple of kids, each scared the other will outdo him."

"That's how people get famous, outdoing everybody else."

The reindeer bones were picked clean, and the dancing continued as the audience drank strong tea. The sun set briefly. When it rose again at half past one, Captain Gillen said, "High tide, boys. Time to go."

Drumming and dancing stopped. The Eskimos took the Mounties in the umiak back to the *St. Roch*. She sailed at two thirty in the morning with Olga standing on the stern howling mournfully toward the shore. All the dogs in the village answered.

Soon after *St. Roch* left Port Clarence, the clear skies and bright sun were befouled by rain and wind. The current still set northerly, and by ten in the morning the ship wallowed around Cape Prince of Wales and into Bering Strait. Later the weather cleared and the *St. Roch* crossed the Arctic Circle in the evening under a blue sky and a warm

47

sun. The ship was out of sight of land, alone in the en-circling Chukchi Sea.

"We're not far from the ice pack," Larsen said.

"How can you tell?" Parsloe asked.

The mate indicated a glow in the northern sky. "That's ice blink. The ice reflects the sun, yust like a mirror."

The fair weather lasted only a few hours, until a sudden gale blew out of the northwest, bringing icy rain and board-ing seas. All through the daylight night the *St. Roch* quar-tered into the swells at half speed. Seasick crewmen shivered under blankets in the cold forecastle. The wind was so strong and gusty a fire wouldn't burn in the heating stove. The gale flattened the crests of the rollers and whipped them into a thick mist blowing low over the water.

"She's sure smokin' today!" said the watch.

After the change of watch at eight A.M. a low spit ap-peared on the sea ahead.

"That'll be Point Hope," the captain said. "I've had enough of this slop. We'll go into the lee and hang on to the hook till it blows over."

An hour later they were anchored in the shelter of a long sandspit that thrust some miles out into the sea. Forecastle and galley fires were relighted. The seasick men recovered quickly, and everyone was hungry when Parry put food on the table.

At noon Seeley called Point Barrow on the wireless. The ice had gone out several days before, but the storm had driven the pack inshore again. Several ships were anchored down the coast waiting for it to recede. They were a trading schooner, the *Patterson,* the *Boxer,* and the *Baychimo*—the Hudson's Bay ship.

The barometer began to rise and the wind moderated in midafternoon. The anchor was heaved and the *St. Roch* got under way with all sails set and engine running. Beyond Point Hope the crew saw the first ice—dirty, rotten stuff stranded on the beach and offshore shoals. A sea was running from the northwest, but when Cape Lisburne was sighted some hours later, the sky was cloudless and the sun was brilliant.

At Lisburne the course was changed to northeast, and the *St. Roch* rode an easy, comfortable swell. After supper everyone came on deck to watch the sparkling ocean seaward and the low green hills inshore. Some stripped to the waist to expose pale skins to the sun.

"I never thought I'd be getting a tan in the middle of the night," one said.

Floating ice was sighted, scattered chunks and small floes awash in the sea. Larsen went to the crow's nest.

"It's moving away from shore!" he called down. He returned to the deck. "If this east wind holds it will all be gone in the morning."

"A piece over there's moving!"

"That's not ice, it's a polar bear."

The course was altered, and they intercepted not one, but two white bears. The second was a cub, teeth in its mother's tail, towing along behind. Cameras appeared and snapshots were taken, then the ship went back on course again.

"We'll see the midnight sun tonight," Captain Gillen said.

The sun moved down until it almost touched the sea, hung there for a few minutes, then began to lift for another circuit of the sky. Gillen consulted the sunrise and sunset tables. "It won't set again until July 27, five days from now."

The wind held steady off the land, and soon the sea was free of ice. Little more was seen until the ship reached Barrow two days later. The ocean beyond this upper tip of Alaska was jammed. The *Boxer* and *Patterson* were anchored off the village unloading into scows and umiaks. The *Baychimo* was moored to the edge of the ice, and the *St. Roch* hove to close by. Gillen hailed the master, Captain Cornwall. "How are things around the point?"

"A few hours ago it looked solid all the way to the Pole."

"Things may have changed. We'll go have a look."

Captain Gillen went to the crow's nest, and the *St. Roch* cruised slowly along the rim of the pack. A hundred yards or so from Point Barrow he ordered the engine stopped. The vessel drifted. After studying the ice for a time, he called for Larsen to come up. Henry went aloft, and Gillen pointed over the bow. "Looks like a weak spot there that might turn into a lead if we rammed it a little. What do you think?"

"The current is holding the pack against the point, but if we got a crack in it, the offshore wind might open it all right."

"We'll give it a try. I'll stay here. You go down and hit that place with everything she's got."

Descending, Henry took the helm. He signaled "Full Ahead." The ship trembled as the engine came to life, and foam kicked out astern.

Larsen spoke into the tube. "Hold on to something down there, boys. We're going to try to bull our way through!"

All hands braced for the shock. The *St. Roch* hit the ice at full tilt. The mainmast snapped like a buggy whip, and Captain Gillen was flung half out of the crow's nest.

"Hold it!" he yelled. "I forgot we don't have any backstays yet!" He tried to open the trapdoor in the bottom of the crow's nest, but it had been jammed shut by the whipping of the mast.

The ramming had opened the ice a bit, but it was closing in around the ship. Floes, carried by the current, banged into the hull and sent tremors up the mainmast.

"Somebody bring up a maul and knock this trapdoor open so I can get out of here!"

A man scrambled up the ratlines, hammered the door open, and hurried down with Captain Gillen close behind. His face was ashen. "I don't want any more of that!"

They backed off and rammed the pack again and again

until a crack opened. The bow thrust into it, the engine ran at full power, and the crack slowly widened. The offshore wind found the split and soon a long, winding lead began to open.

As the *St. Roch* cruised down the passage she had made, the captain said, "I get the creeps every time I pass Point Barrow. It's like walking into a trap."

As they sailed eastward through the Beaufort Sea, the good weather held for two days, then a howler came out of the northwest, the ice moved in, and they were beset. It was July 27 and, as predicted in the tables, the sun set for a few minutes at midnight.

On the afternoon of the third day of imprisonment in the ice, the wind swung around to the south. Soon the sea was clear, and the *St. Roch* got under way again. On July 30 she passed Demarcation Point. "From here on all the land we see is Canada, boys."

A headland soon rose from the sea. "There's Herschel!"

"It's going to be great to get our feet on the ground."

Before long the *St. Roch* was entering a harbor protected by a sandspit on one side and steep cliffs on the other. The *Baychimo* was anchored offshore. Yellow flags flew over the buildings on the spit.

"Quarantine!" Larsen said. "There's disease here!"

[6]

A MOTORBOAT CAME OUT from shore and pulled up alongside. The operator, a tall, lean, blue-eyed man in his early thirties, called up, "I'm Inspector Vernon Kemp. Sorry we can't give you a decent welcome, but we've got an influenza epidemic here." He spoke with the accent of an Englishman.

He said he'd been at Aklavik when the Mackenzie River steamer had arrived with mail, supplies, and passengers from Edmonton. Some of those aboard had bad colds. Returning to Herschel in a power launch, one of the passengers got sick and was put ashore at Shingle Point, a mainland village of about one hundred Eskimos. The launch continued on, and during the day an Eskimo woman became severely ill. Upon arriving at Herschel the sick woman went ashore to visit friends. Two days later the local natives began getting sick. High temperatures and violent chills indicated more than just a common cold. The disease was diagnosed as influenza. Soon every native on the island had it. Responsibility for their care fell to the Mounted Police.

"We've been having an awful time with them," the inspector said "They think the temperature is what makes them sick and not the other way around. We have to watch them or they'll strip and sit out in the wind to cool off. We've buried six already."

"Anything we can do to help, Inspector?"

"Just stay away from everybody so you don't catch it. If we don't stop it here, there won't be an Eskimo left in the Arctic. They have no resistance to it."

"We can unload, can't we?"

"The sooner the better. I want to leave for Cambridge Bay as soon as we can get out of here."

"Is our engineer here?"

"On his way down from Aklavik, at Shingle Point he found everyone sick, the dogs starving, and the dead unburied, so he stayed there to take care of things. We can pick him up on the way east, but we'll have to leave one of your boys there to relieve him." He started the engine of his boat and chugged off to the *Baychimo*.

The water was deep right up to the shore, and the *St. Roch* was moored broadside to the beach. The *Baychimo* came in to lie forward of her. The unloading of both ships began at once. The *Baychimo* used steam winches, and the *St. Roch,* mainly the muscles of her crew.

"Norwegian steam," Larsen said.

Sacks of coal were manhandled to a chute, slid down to the beach, and were carried up and piled above the high-tide line. It was hot, dirty, backbreaking work. Lumber was handed ashore board by board. Barrels of diesel oil were swung over with the winch and rolled up near the coal pile. The Mounties worked until suppertime, rested an hour, then sweated on under the nighttime sun. They saw it set at eleven o'clock and rise again at one.

When the unloading of deck cargo was finished, the crew turned in. They had become accustomed to sleeping with daylight coming through the portholes, but this time they had trouble dropping off because of the clamor of dogs ashore. The howling and barking seemed never to cease.

"You wouldn't need a foghorn to find this place in an overcast," someone grumbled.

"You'd better get used to it. We'll be living with a dozen or so of the noisy brutes all winter."

When they got up for breakfast, the *Patterson* was lying against the beach astern, an old auxiliary schooner with a sawed-off bowsprit. Eskimos were coming and going over a gangplank between the ship and shore.

"Doesn't the quarantine apply to her?" someone asked.

"She won't go beyond here," Gillen said. "There's no danger of her spreading the disease."

A number of small schooners owned by natives and traders were in the harbor too. They came every year to Herschel to meet the ships and sell their furs and buy supplies for the coming year.

Inspector Kemp, standing on the beach beside the *St. Roch* with his wife and small daughter, said, "We're taking a chance letting them land, but we can't send them away without their merchandise. Everyone who hasn't had the disease has to keep away from the local people. We've set up different store hours for them on the *Patterson* and at the Hudson's Bay store to keep them segregated, and the trading is being done in the open. I hope it works. If these schooners carry just one case of flu from here, all our efforts will be wasted. With their ideas about sanitation and cleanliness, the Kogmolliks and other primitive tribes to the east wouldn't have a chance."

A missionary was present, face lined and drawn from sleepless nights spent in nursing duties. Looking up at the crewmen of the *St. Roch,* he said, "Considering the circumstances, your ship is most aptly named."

"What do you mean, Father?"

"Saint Roch is the patron saint of victims of pestilence. He lived in France in the fourteenth century and went to Italy to nurse those stricken with the plague. When he himself caught the disease he was found and brought assistance by a dog." He indicated Olga romping around the deck. "The picture is complete."

54

Captain Gillen spoke to Kemp. "It's nine hundred miles to Cambridge Bay, and the season is late. We're ready to go when you are, Inspector."

"I want to leave in the morning. Things are in fair shape here now. Corporal Kennedy can handle anything that comes up."

The next day was August 1. The inspector, dressed in a fresh uniform, had just brought his kit aboard when he learned that the barometer had dropped abruptly.

"You'd better get away from the beach, Captain," he said. "When the glass falls fast here we're in for a sou'wester."

The *St. Roch* was just pulling away from shore when a vicious gale came whistling in over the bluffs on the northwest side of the harbor. With the first gust several of the small schooners blew ashore. Others were almost sunk.

"I thought you said it would be a sou'wester, Inspector?"

"Don't ask me why, but nor'westers are called sou'westers here!"

They crossed the bay and dropped the hook in the lee of the bluffs. The *Baychimo* and *Patterson* were soon lying nearby, bows into the wind. All three vessels kept propellers turning to lessen the strain on the anchors. Wind-driven water began washing toward the settlement until waves almost reached the doors of the detachment buildings.

After several hours, with no letup in the storm, the coal smoke whipping from the *Baychimo*'s stack got blacker. Men in boots and oilskins went to the windlass on the bow and began to hoist the anchor.

"It looks as if Cornwall is pulling out," Kemp said. "Isn't he taking an awful chance?"

"Every hour he stays here he's taking a chance of not getting to Victoria Land and back around Point Barrow before the pack closes in for the winter," Larsen said.

The steamer headed for sea. Watching, the inspector said, "Do you think it's safe for us to leave too?"

"It's safe enough, sir, if you don't mind a rough ride," said Henry Larsen.

"Don't worry about me. Let's go!"

The anchor was raised and they crossed the harbor. Rounding the sandspit, the *St. Roch* plunged into the combing rollers of the open ocean and went into her dance. Kemp hung on grimly.

"Want to turn back, Inspector?"

Kemp shook his head and gritted his teeth. After a few minutes he said, "I'm afraid I'm getting sick. Where's the W.C.?" After a time there he went to his bunk and was seen no more until the wind died several hours later. He was pale when he returned to the pilothouse.

"I've never been so sick in my life, even on the Atlantic."

"That's no disgrace on here, sir," Larsen chuckled.

Late in the evening they anchored off Shingle Point. Alcide Lamothe, a young recruit with the shortest service, was assigned to take over from Constable Kells the duties of caring for the sick.

"I'm sorry I have to give you such a miserable job," the inspector said, "but the junior man always gets stuck with the dirty work."

The young constable expressed concern about his lack of ability.

"If I didn't think you capable, I wouldn't leave you here. You will be completely on your own, and you'll have a chance to prove to yourself what you *can* do. Once you've bathed and bed-panned a sick Eskimo and buried a dead one you'll be able to do *anything*."

Lamothe was given medical supplies and new clothes to take to Kells. As he waited with his gear while a boat was being lowered, his shipmates came to say good-by. The last was Parry. "Lad, the reputation of the Force was made by men who did things no one ever did before, and without any regulation book or advice from Ottawa. Just roll up your sleeves and go to work. You'll make out all right."

Watching the boat chug toward shore, Kemp said, "I wish he were a little older. He's *so* young."

"But he'll be a man when we get back, sir."

The returning boat brought a tired, unshaven Kells. According to instructions carried ashore by Lamothe, he had bathed and changed clothes and left behind everything he owned.

"How are things?" the inspector asked as the weary Mountie boarded.

"Not too bad now, but that boy has a lot of hungry dogs and sick people to look after. I hope he's got a strong stomach."

"Did you have any deaths?"

"I've buried nine, but I think the rest will make it."

"You look like you've just come out of hell. You'd better go below and have a good long sleep."

"And when you wake up," Parry said, "I'll give you a haircut and a shave. You look more like a grizzly bear than a policeman."

The boat was hoisted aboard, and the *St. Roch* got under way. They steered northeast through the muddy, driftwood-littered water pouring from the channels of the Mackenzie River delta. Lightened of the tonnage left at Herschel, the vessel floated a foot higher and cruised two knots faster. Scattered ice was easily avoided.

The day after leaving Shingle Point, Kells declared himself ready to work. After he assisted the others for a few hours, new engine room watches were set, four hours on and eight off, instead of the six and six Kelly and Foster had been standing.

Three uneventful days later, anchor was dropped at Baillie Island, 350 miles from Shingle Point. There the R.C.M.P. detachment consisted of two, Constables Wall and Fielder. The natives in their care were all healthy-looking. The inspector gave instructions to keep all outsiders away and what to do if the disease should strike. Then he inspected the buildings, audited the books, inventoried stores, and discussed police matters. Coal and supplies were ferried ashore, the crew working twenty-four hours in one stretch to get the job done.

"We can catch up on our rest this winter," wrote Larsen in the log.

Leaving Baillie Island, they found Amundsen Gulf jammed with ice. Gillen ordered the engine stopped. The vessel drifted. The way ahead looked impassable.

Kemp was worried. "What do we do now, go back to Baillie until it clears?"

"That's up to Henry," Gillen said. "He's the ice man."

Larsen studied the pack and looked at the sky. "There are open leads ahead if we can get to them."

Kemp eyed the endless floes. "Where?"

Larsen explained that dark lines on the iceblink indicated the leads. "Light doesn't reflect from open water the way it does from ice. Do you want to wait for a lead to open by itself, or shall we bull our way through?"

"Let's give it a try."

Larsen spoke into the tube. "Stand by for some fast bell work down there. We're going into the pack." To those in the pilothouse he said, "Find something to hang on to. I'm going aloft."

"Don't forget we haven't any backstays, Henry," Gillen warned.

"I won't." He climbed to the crow's nest and watched the ice for some time. It was slowly revolving counterclockwise. Finally he pointed over the starboard bow and called down, "Full ahead, Cap! Hit yust to the right of that hummock!" He braced himself as the vibration of the speeding engine made the mainmast quiver.

Kemp held on to the binnacle. The *St. Roch* plowed toward the pack. "We aren't going to ram at full speed are we?"

"You want to get through, don't you?" Gillen said, hanging on.

"Yes, but it's taken years to get this ship. If anything happens to her, Commissioner Starnes will have my scalp."

"Starnes is in Ottawa. Hang on!"

The place picked for the *St. Roch*'s encounter with the ice was a floe tilting down into the sea. Moments before her steel-shod forefoot struck the sloping shelf, Larsen ordered the engine stopped. Carried by momentum, she slid half her length onto the floe, coming to rest with bow canted upward and stern low in the water.

"Port the helm and full ahead!"

Olsen put the wheel hard left, and the throttle was opened. Keel grinding on the ice, the stern swung to the right.

"Hard astarboard!" The stern swung the other way, there was a loud, "Crack!" and the floe broke in two. The *St. Roch* settled into the water on an even keel again.

"Midship the rudder and full astern!" The ship backed out of the opening she had made, then rammed forward again, further splitting the ice. Full astern, full ahead, over and over again. Soon the lead was opening of its own accord, nudged now and again by the ship.

"So that's how it's done," Kemp said when Larsen came down for coffee.

"Yah. Yust find a weak spot and give it a little help."

Hour upon hour they cruised the leads through shifting ice. Larsen only left the crow's nest to come down for a quick cup of coffee and a sandwich, a turn around the deck to stretch his legs, and he was up the mast again.

"That man is fabulous," the inspector said to Gillen.

"One of the best."

Occasionally a lead closed, but they rammed on through to another stretch of open water. Once the ship got stuck and could go neither forward nor astern.

Henry came down. "I guess we'll have to bomb."

Several bombs were made—five pounds of black powder in a tin can fitted with a fuse. Larsen and Olsen went out on the ice ahead of the ship. Two bombs, attached to long poles, were planted several yards apart, deep in a crack. The fuses were lighted. The bombs exploded with a flash of fire, a boom, and a cloud of black smoke. Shattered ice was still falling when Gillen rammed the *St. Roch* into the blasted opening. She hung up again, but the detonation of two more bombs opened the way to another lead. The bombardiers scrambled aboard, and Larsen returned to the masthead.

Late in the day a current coming out of Franklin Bay closed the leads and the ship was solidly beset. Larsen returned to the deck. "All we can do is drift with the ice and see what happens."

Sitting in the chart room after supper, Inspector Kemp said, "After seeing how helpless a modern ship like this can be in the ice, I'm really amazed by what the early-day explorers accomplished with their windjammers. I guess they were lucky."

"You can't count on luck in the Arctic," Gillen said. "The only reason any of those old ships came back at all was because they had good masters."

"What made them good—besides seamanship, of course?"

"Patience and courage—patience to sit beset or frozen in for years, and courage to take a chance when things looked right. Humans are single-minded. This continent was discovered by people trying to get to India. Instead of looking for riches in America, all they could think of was to find a way around and get on to India. I guess that's why so many went searching for a Northwest Passage."

"Yah, and it was four hundred years before Amundsen made it." Larsen sat looking out at the ice pack and the clouding sky for a time. Finally he spoke. "You know, sir, I'd like to put *this* ship through the Northwest Passage someday. She's built to take it. I believe she could make it."

[7]

IT WAS RAINING HARD, and the *St. Roch* was still beset when Parsloe came on watch at midnight. A low headland was barely visible through the drizzle a couple of miles astern. Larsen was in the chart room.

"Where are we, Henry?"

"Yust coming up on Cape Parry."

"We've passed it. It's astern."

Larsen grinned and shook his head. "The pack is revolving. We're headed west but drifting east."

"I'm sure turned around." Parsloe looked at the map of Canada and Arctic regions tacked to the bulkhead. "Where are we on here?"

"About 71 degrees north latitude and 125 degrees west longitude—right there." Larsen put a finger on the map.

Parsloe traced the 125th degree of longitude downward. "Why, we're still west of Vancouver. We've been at sea six weeks, cruised 3,500 miles, and we're *still* west of Vancouver!"

"Yah, and 1,500 miles north. It was a long way around Alaska."

By two o'clock the ice had revolved until the bow was pointing east again. Cape Parry was over the starboard beam, directly to the south. Larsen went to the masthead for a look. Returning, he said, "There's open water in Darnley

Bay. If there's a current coming out of there, it should open some leads."

"I hope so," Parsloe said. "I'm sick of doing nothing."

"I've got a yob for you. There's pools of rainwater on the ice. Get on your oilskins and boots and we'll start filling the fresh-water tanks."

"Me and my big mouth!"

Parsloe carried buckets of water from a pool forward of the ship. Larsen pulled them up with a line and poured them into the fill pipe. It took the rest of the watch to top off the forward tank. Olsen took over at four o'clock, and they began to fill the after tank. Cape Parry was astern, and less than a mile of ice lay between the *St. Roch* and open water, when Olsen came hurrying back, slithering on the slippery floe. He threw the buckets clattering onto the deck and scrambled over the bulwark. "The ice is moving!"

"Yah, I felt it." Larsen alerted the engineers to stand by, then went aloft.

The current setting out of Darnley Bay was nibbling at the edge of the pack and marching chunks of ice off to the east. All around, the floes were cracking apart and starting to move. Everyone came on deck, roused by the smashing and grinding against the hull. Every movement came up to Larsen, perched in the crow's nest, magnified by the pendulum action of the tall mainmast. He wished they had taken time to get it backstayed.

The vessel shook violently, and a crack opened in front of the bow. "Full ahead!" The mast trembled with the vibration of the diesel engine, and the ship pressed into the crack, widening it.

"Hard astarboard! Hard aport!" The stern kicked left and right; the crack widened and became a lead. Soon the *St. Roch* was out of the pack and cruising through the ice pans that streamed eastward.

Beyond Cape Lyon, Amundsen Gulf was full of ice except for a strip of open water near the shore. Larsen directed that the ship be headed there and soundings be taken. As she skirted the ice a hundred yards offshore, the leadsman found no bottom at ten fathoms. East of the cape the ice veered northward and the channel widened.

Keeping the ship close to the pack to take advantage of the current, Gillen had the sails set to catch the wind coming off the hills that rimmed the shoreline to the south. He took bearings. "We're making ten knots over the ground."

Larsen kept the leadsman busy. "You never know when an ice yam might have built a sandbar someplace," he said. "The worst thing you can do is go aground and be run down by the pack."

The weather cleared, and the sun came out. While Larsen had his lunch, Tudor went to the masthead. Coming down again, he reported land off to the north.

"That will be Cape Baring on Victoria Land," Henry said. "We're in Dolphin and Union Strait now. The current is easterly here, so if we get beset, we'll keep drifting."

"Have you been in Coronation Gulf?" the inspector asked.

"Oh, enough to find my way around all right."

"I understand there's a fellow at Inman River who's been sailing these waters for some years. I was wondering if it might not be wise to hire him to pilot us to Cambridge Bay and back. It's no reflection on your ability, but a local skipper should know his way around."

"Yah. He wouldn't last long up here if he didn't."

Shortly after sunrise at two the following morning, the *St. Roch* anchored off the mouth of the Inman River. Inspector Kemp was taken ashore in a boat. As at Baillie Island, he warned the people of the epidemic and how to avoid it. He found the owner of a small schooner moored near the native village. Yes, the shaggy mariner said he knew the waters between here and Cambridge Bay like the inside of his hat. Sure, he would be glad to pilot the *St. Roch* there and back. An agreement was made, and he brought his gear aboard.

They raised anchor and sailed with the Inman River pilot at the helm. He steered a course close in, parallel to the shore.

Larsen frowned. "Shouldn't we be farther out, Captain?"

"I've sailed my boat through here a hundred times, Mate."

"I'd feel better if I knew how deep it is." He told Olsen to go heave the lead. He had hardly given the order when the *St. Roch* hit a reef and shuddered to a stop. When he had stopped the engine Larsen said, "What's the draft of that boat of yours, Captain?"

"Eight feet."

"We're drawing twelve forward and thirteen aft."

Kemp hurried to the wheelhouse. "What happened?"

"We ran out of water, sir," Larsen said.

"Do you think we're damaged?"

"We won't know till we get her off." He signaled for the engine to be run full astern. The ship trembled, and muddy water boiled from under the counter. He turned the wheel right and left, but nothing happened. He stopped the engine. "We're really on."

"Maybe the tide will float us off."

"There's hardly any tide here. We'll have to shift cargo."

All hands, including the inspector, turned to. They carried the coal remaining on the well deck aft to lighten the bow and weight the stern down. Again, nothing happened. Soundings indicated the vessel was two thirds of her length onto the reef.

"Lighten ship!"

Timbers were put overside and lashed together to form a floating pen. The drums of oil were dumped into it. They had just enough buoyancy to float an inch or two above the water. Most of the fresh water was pumped overboard. Even when lightened by many tons the *St. Roch* wouldn't budge. They tried to kedge her off by carrying the anchors to deep water with the boats, dropping them, and winding in the chains with the windlass. They heaved until the clutches smoked and the machinery threatened to pull from its mountings.

"It won't work."

"What do we do now," Kemp asked, "discharge the hold?"

"Yah, but let's wait till the boys get some rest first."

For a day and a half since the grounding everyone had been working without letup.

"And what if *that* doesn't work?"

"The *Baychimo* is only about a hundred miles away," Gillen said. "We can wireless her to come pull us off."

The last thing the inspector wanted was to call for help on the *St. Roch*'s first trip. Too many listened in to the wireless—he didn't want Commissioner Starnes, head of the R.C.M.P., to learn of the predicament until it had been corrected. "He told me before I left Ottawa what this ship would cost and what it means to the Force. If we lose her, he'll have me counting fire extinguishers in the Government Building for the rest of my career."

"If we don't get her afloat, we'll lose her for sure," Larsen said.

"And under admiralty law," Gillen said, "if we are in danger and the *Baychimo* saves us, she'll be entitled to claim salvage."

"Well, regardless of my reputation or salvage we can't lose this boat. I'll send Cornwall a message not to leave the area without contacting us. He'll probably figure we're in trouble." Kemp had Seeley send a carefully worded message, and received an answer that the *Baychimo* would contact the *St. Roch* before leaving. "I guess all we can do now is get some rest, then start unloading."

"If I were one of those superstitious sailormen," Larsen said, "I'd try to whistle up a wind."

"I'd think the last thing we'd want now is wind," protested Kemp.

"A northerly might raise the water enough to float us off." The mate went forward, whistling softly to himself.

65

Kemp asked Gillen if *he* thought that whistling could bring wind.

"I've gone to sea too long to whistle if I *don't* want wind."

There was a lot of controversy later about whether Henry did "whistle up a wind" that day, or if it was just another sudden Arctic blow that came roaring down Dolphin and Union Strait, raising the water enough to float the *St. Roch* off the reef.

When she was in deep water, regardless of wind and chilling rain, aching bones and weary muscles, everyone turned to with a will to reload the oil barrels and manhandle the coal back where it belonged. Soon they were under way again. The lead was kept going the rest of the way to Bernard Harbour except when the ship was well offshore in waters known by Larsen to be safe. The pilot offered no advice unless it was asked of him.

The Bernard Harbour detachment was inspected, supplies were unloaded, and the natives instructed in precautions against influenza. Sergeant E. G. Baker, who was in charge, was told to bring his gear aboard for transfer to Cambridge Bay, where he was to replace Sergeant Fred Anderton. Anderton, an experienced northerner, would be in charge of the police duties of the *St. Roch* detachment.

Baker was concerned about two handicapped Eskimos in his care. One, Oluksak, had been imprisoned some years earlier for the murder of two Catholic priests. Since release he had become afflicted with tuberculosis. The other man, old, blind, feeble, and a burden to his people, had been abandoned on the ice to die. A white trader had found the old man, loaded him on his dogsled, and turned him over to the Mounted Police. Kemp agreed to stop on the way back from Cambridge Bay, pick up the blind man and the sick murderer, and take them to Herschel Island for transfer to the Anglican hospital at Aklavik.

It took a week to navigate the four hundred miles through

Coronation Gulf and Dease Strait to Cambridge Bay. The *Baychimo* was there. When her crew learned the reason for Kemp's message, the *St. Roch's* men came in for a bit of ribbing. The Inman River pilot stayed pretty much to himself except to go to the trading post ashore and buy his year's allowance of two gallons of rum.

Some of the detachment men bought rum too, in stone jugs, and part of their winter clothing.

Sergeant Anderton was looking forward to his new duties. A floating detachment was unique for the Mounted Police, and he was anxious to prove its worth. Besides freeing the Force from dependency on private vessels for transport of supplies and personnel, the ship could be sent to isolated regions where temporary governmental representation was desired, but where the expense of a permanent detachment was not warranted.

The inspection and transfer of command was soon effected. Two Kogmolliks, a man and a woman, were to be returned to Aklavik to be tried for murder. One crime was the result of an ancient Eskimo practice of putting newborn girls to death. Boys grew up to be hunters, valuable to the tribe. Girls produced more unwanted mouths to be fed. Only enough were allowed to live to perpetuate a family. Eventually there were so few women that often each had two or more husbands. The female prisoner had eliminated a spouse she considered unneeded.

The male prisoner, Okchina, allegedly had murdered Oksuk, a bad-tempered "medicine man," at the instigation of Oksuk's wife and others to prevent further cruelty to her. The prisoners, their relatives, and the witnesses were brought aboard. They set up camp on the well deck, all happily looking forward to the voyage.

When the police schooner cruised slowly out of Cambridge Bay, the *Baychimo* blew a farewell blast on her whistle. The *St. Roch* answered with a toot of her air horn, then veered from the channel and grounded gently in the shallows. The English crew of the Hudson's Bay ship howled and hooted. "Saint R-o-c-k!" someone yelled.

Larsen and Kemp were on the fantail. "Who's at the wheel?" the inspector demanded, red with anger.

"The pilot, sir."

"What's the matter with him, anyway?"

Larsen went to see and reported back, "He's pickled to the gills."

"Get him below! Who assigned him to the helm, anyway?"

"Captain Gillen, sir."

"Where is he?"

"I'm afraid he's been drinking too."

"All right, from here on you're in complete charge of navigation. See if you can get her afloat without any help."

At slow speed, the *St. Roch* hadn't grounded very hard. After a few minutes of running the engine full astern and maneuvering the rudder some, Larsen broke her free of the bottom and backed her into the channel. With no damage other than to her dignity, she continued seaward as the inspector muttered, "If you want a job done right, it takes the Mounted Police to do it."

He told Jack Foster to see if he could find where Captain Gillen's jug was hidden. Jack knew where it was—in the sail locker with his own jug, which was almost empty. He poured the rum remaining in Gillen's jug into his own, then went topside and threw Gillen's empty one overboard. "There it is, Inspector!"

The voyage back to Herschel was without incident. The weather was worsening, gales came more often, and the pack ice thickened. Fog and rain increased, and little sun was seen. The time between sunset and sunrise lengthened daily. Night was six hours long, with semidarkness during the midnight hours when stars appeared again in clear weather.

The vessel stopped at Bernard Harbour to pick up the blind old cripple and the tubercular murderer. A tent was pitched over one of the motorboats, and they set up house-keeping. Larsen liked Eskimos and spent a lot of time trying to learn their difficult language. Speaking to Larsen on the stern, Oluksak said in his prison-learned pidgin English, "Hey, maybe you talk Canadian, eh? You say Eskimo funny."

"Yah." Larsen grinned and switched to English.

"Hey, you say Canadian funny too!"

They stopped at Inman River, paid off the pilot in supplies, and put him and his remaining rum ashore.

The *St. Roch* called briefly at each village where she had stopped on the outbound voyage. There had been no sickness anywhere. Kemp was elated. "I guess we stopped it, all right." At Shingle Point, Lamothe reported no more deaths. The survivors were in good health again. At Herschel Island an epidemic-free community greeted the *St. Roch* on August 24.

The Eskimos were moved ashore to await transfer to Aklavik. Pat Kelly and Captain Gillen took quarters at the R.C.M.P. detachment to await arrival of the *Baychimo*, on which they would return to Vancouver. The steamer, expected early in September, was working through the ice from Cambridge Bay in a race to get around Point Barrow before the pack closed in.

Summer would be on the calendar for another month, but a bite was already in the air, and everyone was preparing for winter. Eskimos netted fish and hunted seals. The policemen of the permanent detachment reinforced their buildings and made repairs with lumber brought by the *St. Roch*. Trappers and traders in motorboats and schooners darted in to sell furs, buy supplies, and hurry away again.

Since the danger of the epidemic was past, the crew was allowed the freedom of the shore. There was little to see but the detachment buildings and small native village, the Hudson's Bay post, and an Anglican mission. Nor was there time for much sightseeing and visiting away from the vessel.

Long service in the Arctic had made Sergeant Anderton a

believer in thorough preparation. "It's easier to stay out of trouble than to get out of trouble." Painting, cleaning, and repairing was the order of the day, every day. "Keep the boys busy," he said, "and they'll have no time for mischief."

Inspector Kemp decided that the *St. Roch* would spend her first winter at Langton Bay, 350 miles to the east at the southern end of Franklin Bay. "There's lots of fish and game there and a good fresh water supply. It's protected from the pack, and breakup is usually early, so you won't be frozen in all next summer. It's remote enough to be a good test of being on your own, yet it's only a hundred miles to Baillie Island and 250 overland to Aklavik in case anything happens and you need help."

He made the permanent crew assignments, with Anderton in overall charge of the detachment and Larsen as navigator. Tudor was appointed first mate, with Olsen second mate. Jack Foster was chief engineer and Kells the assistant. Dad Parry, of course, was cook, and Seeley wireless operator. At the end of navigation all but Parry and Seeley would function as regular Mounted Policemen.

By August 30, 1928, everything had been done that needed doing at Herschel Island. Thirteen huskies, including Larsen's Olga, were dragged snarling and barking aboard and chained, each out of reach of its neighbor's snapping teeth. Two komatiks, basket sleds, dog feed, and harnesses were loaded. A farewell toot of the whistle set the hundreds of dogs ashore to howling. They drowned out the sound of wind in the rigging and the snapping of the Union Jack astern.

The day after departure Seeley received a wireless report that a float from Amundsen's airplane had been found in the sea not far from Tromso, Norway, where it had taken off more than two months earlier.

"That's tough, Henry," Seeley said.

"Yah." He went aloft and spent the remainder of the day in the crow's nest.

[8]

WITH THE SOUTHWARD SWING of the sun, temperatures dropped in the Arctic. The polar ice pack, earlier broken and shrunk by perpetual sunlight, was congealing again and expanding. Loose floes on its rim were carried off by currents. Such free ice, streaming from the Beaufort Sea into Amundsen Gulf, slowed the *St. Roch*'s final voyage of the season. But the crew had become accustomed to drifting with the pack while waiting a chance to ram and blast to open water. Nine days after leaving Herschel Island they anchored near the north side of Langton Bay where a curving sandspit gave protection from northerlies and drifting floes.

Larsen wasn't satisfied with the holding ground. Samples brought up in the hole in the bottom of the sounding lead were mostly sand. "It may be all right, but we won't know whether the anchors will drag until we've had a good blow."

He was not concerned about a good water supply. The men had found a clean lake two miles inland. When it had frozen to a thickness of one foot, blocks of ice would be cut and sledded to the ship for melting. It would take forty tons to see them through the winter. They set nets in the lake for trout, and caught salt water fish with hook and line over the side of the ship.

The first days were bright and warm, but the temperature

dropped sharply at sunset. Hard skims of ice on nearby ponds in the mornings melted in the afternoons. The surrounding land was barren hills and swampy lowlands.

"I'm glad we didn't get here earlier," Anderton said. "This is mosquito country."

He had the men dig several pails of mud ashore and bring them to the ship. He said this was for sled runners.

The first step in preparing for the winter was to lighten ship so she would be floating high when frozen in and there would be less hull under pressure of the ice. Oil and coal were taken ashore, and spare clothes, bedding, and emergency stores were cached there against the possibility of the vessel's being lost to ice or fire.

Ten days after she reached winter quarters, a southerly struck the *St. Roch* so abruptly that she was blown, with anchors dragging, broadside onto the sandspit. When the storm died and the wind-driven water dropped to normal, there was no more than four feet of depth anywhere along her length.

"Do you think we can get her afloat, Henry?" Anderton asked.

"We'd better, or the R.C.M.P. has a permanent detachment here."

The situation looked hopeless to Anderton. "Well, you're the man who has to figure out how to get us off the beach. I'm a landsman, and I haven't the slightest idea how to do it."

Larsen studied the predicament for a time, took soundings over each side of the grounded vessel, and conferred with Tudor and Olsen. "Yah, I think we can get her off. We'll lighten her as much as we can, then set the yib and fores'l. A good northerly should swing her into deep water."

Everything that could be moved by man or machinery was taken to the sandspit in the boats. Empty barrels were filled with oil from the fuel tanks and sent ashore. There were thirty tons of loose coal in the hold and only twenty sacks to put it in. The twenty were filled, taken to the beach and dumped, brought back and filled again and again until the coal was all unloaded.

They tried kedging, but it didn't work. The deck machinery wasn't powerful enough to swing the bow around.

"We'll just have to wait for that norther."

The ship lay east and west. The jib and foresail were hoisted and set amidships, their surfaces to north and south. "When it blows she'll either flip around like a weathercock or that foremast will snap." Everybody began whistling for a wind.

It came a day and a half later, a first-rate howler straight out of the north, bitterly cold and vicious. At the first gust the foremast shivered and the *St. Roch* heeled. With a shudder the bow broke from the sand, swung away from the beach, and floated. No one cheered. The stern was still fast aground.

The engine was started, but the propeller only churned the shallows to a boil of mud. The sheets were paid out so jib and foresail could catch the full force of the wind. The mainsail was raised. The canvas bellied and snapped, the rigging sang, the masts creaked, but the stern stayed hard aground.

"What now?"

"We'll flood the bow."

The fresh-water tanks were drained into the bilges. The ship was already down by the head, and the water ran forward, weighting the bow deeper. The stern still clung to the bottom.

"Open the sea cocks!"

Kells opened the valves, and the sea gushed into the engine room. At the controls, Foster watched the muddy water rise above the floorplates and felt the bow sink deeper. "If she doesn't come off soon, we're going to get wet!"

Without warning, the stern broke from the bottom and the *St. Roch* slid off the beach. The stern settled, the bow bobbed up. The water swept aft through the engine room in a tidal wave, carrying grease and oil, dirty rags, and other debris that had collected in the bilges. The spinning fly-wheel picked up the oily water and trash and spattered it onto the walls and ceiling.

"Shut her off!" Kells yelled. "Look what it's doing to our paintwork!"

"Not until we get a bell! Start the pumps!"

No signal to stop the engine was received until the ship was well away from the spit and anchored with bow into the norther. When he finally got the bell to shut off the engine, Jack looked around. Goo dripped from the overhead and oozed down the bulkheads. "It will give us something to do this winter, cleaning it up."

"And it's going to take us all winter to do it, too."

The gale blew for three days. Then they cruised around, searching for better holding ground. When it was found they began reloading the cargo taken off after the grounding.

"I volunteered for this duty so I wouldn't have to clean stables," Parsloe said.

"Yes, but look at the big muscles you're getting."

They were still reloading when a small schooner sailed into the bay and came alongside. She was manned by Eskimos from Dogfish Bay, a few miles up the coast. The captain spoke English well, said he had learned it on American whaling ships as a young man. "Why you got all that stuff ashore?" They told him about the grounding. "You should have waited and let the big tide float you off."

"There's no tides to speak of in the Western Arctic."

"Just before freeze-up you always get a big high tide here."

When everything was back aboard and stowed, the sails and running rigging were stripped from the masts and stowed in the sail locker. Then a stout wooden framework was built over the ship from bow to stern and covered with canvas.

"It wasn't the cold that used to kill the old-timers," Larsen said. "They sealed up their ships to keep the heat in, and their breaths and sweat froze to everything. Sailors used to freeze to death in their bunks five feet from a red-hot stove. You have to let the moisture out or your living quarters will frost up like a refrigerator. Now we can leave the skylights open so the dampness will get out."

A few days later another storm ripped part of the canvas off, filled the deck with fine, dry snow, and turned the hills and tundra white. On the third day of the blow the tide rose several feet above normal. For a time waves threatened to wash over the sandspit and carry away the supplies cached there. At the crest of the tide the wind began to fail.

"If that old Eskimo was right, the freeze-up is just around the corner," Olsen said.

The Eskimo *was* right. As the storm ended, the freak tide dropped and the temperature went down to zero and below. Soon the *St. Roch* was locked in a sheet of smooth ice. Beyond the sandspit, Franklin Bay was surfaced with jumbled floes blown there by the storm.

There was no autumn at Langton Bay. It had been summer the day the storm began. It was winter when the storm ended. The last of the insects ashore were gone. All the birds had fled but owls and ravens. The inland lake froze to the desired depth, and the men began cutting ice for water. The dogs were harnessed and the sleds prepared to haul the ice.

"These steel-shod runners pull too hard through dry snow," Sergeant Anderton said. "We'll use a trick I learned from the Kogmolliks." He heated a pail of mud, and with a piece of bearskin he smeared a coating on the runners. It froze instantly to a hard, glassy surface that slid effortlessly in the snow. "If a chunk of mud breaks off, you can use oatmeal mush or flour."

A line was rigged on the ice near the ship where the dogs were tied when they were not working. A snowhouse was built for each. They were fed once a day, a dried fish and a chunk of beef tallow. When seals could be taken the dogs got blubber instead of the tallow.

The storm-damaged canvas deck covering was repaired and nailed down with battens to prevent its blowing loose again. The water tanks, piping, and engine cooling system were drained to prevent freezing damage. The heads were cut from two oil drums, and one was put in the forecastle, the other, in the after living quarters. Each day a man was detailed to keep them filled with ice, heat water on the stoves, then pour it over the ice to melt it for drinking and washing. Anderton and Larsen moved from their stateroom to bunks aft, where it was warmer than the topside quarters.

October came in with a violent southerly that filled the air with a smother of fine, dry snow, the result of wet winds of the central continent blowing into the north. Most of the snow whipped right on by to come to earth somewhere beyond, then to be driven back later by northerlies.

They soon came. Nature, like a logger come from the woods to town, seemed to have chosen October for a prolonged spree before settling down for the winter. For most of the month the weather was foul, with sub-zero temperatures and wild winds from all around the compass. The men stayed below decks for days, except for quick ventures out in mukluks, fur pants, and parkas to feed the dogs and bring in ice for water. Some thought it was a good time to catch up on the rest lost during navigation and to store energy for work to come.

Sergeant Anderton thought otherwise. "You're not here to get fat and hibernate for the winter," he told two who went back to their bunks one morning after breakfast. "This is an R.C.M.P. detachment, not a bear den!" He set up a schedule of duties for everyone, laid down strict rules for house-keeping and personal cleanliness, and enforced them. "Men can turn into pigs when there aren't women around to keep them on their toes. It's not going to happen here—I'm your mother."

With November the winds died and the dark clouds vanished. Like animals peering cautiously from their burrows, the Mounties looked out of the snowed-in ship. Squinting against the dazzling sunlight, they saw a changed scene. Beyond the sandspit the ice on Franklin Bay was smooth now, crevices and hollows filled with snow and planed off by cutting blizzards. Drifts had piled up around the *St. Roch* until she was only a hummock set with ice-rimed masts and rigging and smoking stovepipes. The weak sun in its brief daily passage across the low southern sky cast thousand-foot shadows of the masts upon the ice. Men's shadows reached out a hundred feet, and the dogs' more than thirty.

Anderton ordered everyone to leave the ship and go walking for at least two hours one day each week. "You've got to keep in shape. If anything happens to this ship there's only one way out—on foot."

One or two took their walks reluctantly, did not go far, and returned when the two hours were up. Others went willingly and at every chance. Anderton and Foster usually traveled together, and Larsen went with Olsen.

At first they did not go beyond sight of the crow's nest atop the mainmast, racing over the ice and into the hills with komatiks and dog teams. Gaining experience and stamina, they ventured farther, making overnight trips in search of polar bears and breathing holes in the sea ice where seals might be taken. Much time was spent hunting caribou, but they were scarce. There were wolf sign and sinister nightly howling in the hills which disturbed the dogs and made men uneasy.

Before starting on a trip, the travelers spent a day preparing. To a five-gallon pot of beans was added bacon or other

77

meat, canned tomatoes, onions, molasses, sugar, salt, and mustard. Boiled until it was thick, the mixture was poured into pans and set out to freeze, then chopped into small pieces and bagged in canvas pouches. Doughnuts were fried and frozen. Tea and coffee, rolled oats, and raw frozen fish were loaded on the sled as well as dried fish and canned tallow or blubber for the dogs. Caribou-skin sleeping robes, a primus stove and kerosine, rifles, and a snow knife completed the outfit.

Anderton taught his men the tricks of Arctic living he had learned from Eskimos and other northerners, and Larsen passed on a few that he knew. At the end of a day's travel they made camp in the lee of a drift of hard-packed snow. When the dogs had been fed each man would chew on a piece of raw frozen fish. It made them feel warm and pleasant.

"I don't know why," the sergeant said, "but the natives say it forces warm blood from your insides out to your skin and that's what makes you feel warm."

They carried no tents, which were bulky and heavy, but built a snowhouse each night. While snow melted for tea water on the primus stove, blocks were cut from the drift with the knife and piled in a spiral to a rounded apex. After chinking the crevices with loose snow to keep drafts out, they crawled inside and "closed the door" with snow blocks. With outer garments removed and mukluks taken off and turned inside out to dry, they stretched out on sleeping robes, gulped hot tea, and had a smoke while waiting for the evening meal to thaw in a bucket over the blue flame of the hissing stove.

The primus and men's body heat soon warmed the hut until a vent had to be opened to prevent its melting and collapsing. This was an experience that usually happened once to every man, but only once. Having to crawl from under a heap of broken snow blocks and rebuild a house in the middle of a bitter night made him forever watchful for drippings.

The men learned to stalk the wary, dangerous polar bear. When sign of one was found, the dogs were turned loose to track it down and keep it at bay until the hunters came and shot it. They kept the skin and used all the meat but the liver, which was said to be poisonous. Everything edible was taken back to the ship to be eaten fried.

Seals could be shot at breathing holes when they came up for air, but they often sank and were lost. Few of the Mounties acquired the patience of a native to stand for hours by a hole in the ice, spear upraised, for the moment's opportunity to thrust when the animal appeared. The few that were taken were stripped of skin and blubber and the flesh fried, boiled, or roasted. It had no fishy taste, but always turned black when cooked.

The men wondered how the seals' breathing holes were kept open when the surrounding ice was ten feet thick.

"He has to come up for air about every eight minutes," Larsen said. "He will have several holes and use a different one each time. When he comes up he breaks through the ice that formed since the last time he was there, so it never has a chance to get very thick."

On a trip into the hills, Anderton and Foster spotted a small herd of caribou. They shot eight and dressed them out. Loading three onto the sled, they buried the remaining carcasses in the snow and hurried back to Langton Bay. Before they could return, a storm came up that confined them to the ship for a week. When they got back to the cache they found only tufts of hair and particles of bones and hooves. The wolves had been there.

Some set traps for white fox and snowshoe rabbits, but anything caught was usually devoured by the wolves or owls and ravens.

Though a far better month than October, November had

its periods of sudden violence. Occasionally men were caught out on the ice or in the hills by storms and forced to remain for days in snowhouses. These were times for the testing of character. Some became nervous and cranky, swearing that if they ever got back to the ship they would never leave it again. Others, like Larsen and Olsen, Anderton and Foster, took it as a great experience and usually came back with a new trick or two they had learned.

When daily duties were completed, much leisure time remained aboard the *St. Roch*. Most of it was spent reading, listening to the radio, and playing cards. The Mounties "shot a lot of breeze" too, talking of past experiences. Everyone had a favorite subject. Jack Foster liked to discuss girls. With others it was cars or horses. Dad Parry occasionally mentioned his boyhood days in Wales, and sometimes Sergeant Anderton talked about his experiences when he was a policeman back in England. Henry Larsen usually just listened to the others. Some of the stories they told were ribald, and the subtle jokes of the Englishmen often "went over his head."

When Larsen did talk it was usually about the Arctic, its explorers, and its mysteries. He knew the sagas of the Norsemen—Eric the Red's tenth-century colonization of Greenland, the voyage of his son, Leif Ericson, to North America, and the establishment of settlements in Vinland. "Nobody knows exactly where Vinland was—probably in Newfoundland or Labrador. After a few thousand settlers had been brought to Greenland and Vinland, no more Viking ships came for several hundred years. When they came back, all the people were gone."

"What do you suppose became of them, Henry?"

"They might have turned into Eskimos. Most of the Greenlanders look like they might have white blood in them."

"Speaking of mysteries, I wonder what happened to Franklin?"

"That's no mystery. They got caught in the ice in M'Clintock Channel, and everybody starved."

Two British naval vessels, the *Terror* and *Erebus,* carrying 129 men and officers under the command of Sir John Franklin, sailed in 1845 to find a Northwest Passage or disprove its existence. They were last seen by a whaling ship in Baffin Bay in July of 1845. When the ships did not return on schedule, sixteen different expeditions went in search of them. It was not until 1859 that the mystery was solved.

The yacht *Fox,* commanded by Captain Francis M'Clintock, left Aberdeen, Scotland, in July of 1857 to look for Franklin. Two years later a party from the *Fox* found articles carried by Sir John's men and equipment of his ships in the possession of Boothia Peninsula natives. Skeletons were later found on King William Island, and records discovered at Point Victory gave details of the lost expedition.

The *Terror* and *Erebus* had sailed westward into Barrow Strait, then south through Peel Sound. In September they were stopped by the pack. Still icebound on April 22, 1848, the ships were abandoned, and the crews struck out on foot. Nine officers and fifteen men had already perished, including Franklin, who had died the previous June. The last entry of the record was for April 25. An Eskimo woman had seen the starving, scurvy-ridden men. They staggered as they walked, and one by one fell down and died.

Franklin, a battle-seasoned officer of His Majesty's Navy, had made his first voyage to the Arctic in 1818. The following year he led a company of men overland to explore the northern coast of Canada eastward from the mouth of the Coppermine River. After covering over five thousand miles, they returned to England by way of Hudson Bay.

Returning to the Arctic, from 1825 to 1827 Franklin headed an expedition that charted the coast from the Mackenzie River to the 150th meridian on the northern shore of Alaska. Another member of the party, John Richardson, traced the Canadian coast from the Coppermine to the Mackenzie.

"Why, they must have gone right past here."

"Yah. Old Franklin saw about all the Northwest Passage, but most of it was on foot."

On November 25 a weak sun peeped briefly over the southern skyline, cast miles-long shadows of the masts across the ice for a few minutes, then set for the year. According to the tables it wouldn't rise until January 18, 1929.

The Arctic was not plunged into total darkness. In mid-morning a glow appeared in the southern sky, waning in the early afternoon. In its visible phases the moon never set, but circled endlessly. When full, it lighted frozen land and sea with almost noonday brightness.

During full moon the Mounties made patrols to isolated villages to take the census, check food supplies, and see that the Northwest Territories game laws were not being violated. The Eskimos were not expected to observe the rules to the letter when obtaining animals for food and clothing. They were advised not to kill the caribou unnecessarily or to waste the skins and meat.

Not many years earlier, all hunting in the region had been done with bows and arrows. This permitted the natives to satisfy their requirements, but did not deplete the game. When they obtained firearms, the primitive, often childlike Eskimos, were inclined to use their weapons on anything they saw. In many areas the game was soon wiped out. Only firm enforcement and instructions by the Mounted Police prevented complete extermination of the caribou and musk-oxen.

The larger game was still scarce, and some natives faced starvation. When the Mounties visited the tribes, they carried emergency supplies on the komatiks for distribution to the destitute.

Patrols were also carried on under the northern lights. The aurora borealis was present most of the time, but most vivid during the dark of moon. Some men thought they could hear a sound like rustling silk when the deep-red and pale-green curtains of light swept the heavens. Others said what they were hearing was only the bloodstream flowing through the vessels of their ears. When blindfolded, those who claimed to hear the lights heard nothing.

A sound that everyone could hear was the sharp "Choong!" of ice splitting from the expansion of its freezing. The split could be heard coming from a distance. When it struck, the ship seemed to jump a foot. More ominous were the creakings of the vessel's frame as ice pressure increased against the hull. She was no longer floating, but was as solid as though in concrete.

December was the dark month, but each day there was enough light to travel by for several hours. When winter began, the *St. Roch* had already been frozen in for three months. The thought of another six was depressing. Sergeant Anderton was pressed to keep men occupied, and thankful for the wireless and radio. With the wireless he could keep in contact with headquarters and exchange messages and news with other detachments and Hudson's Bay posts all through the North. The radio helped while away the idle hours and kept them up to date on happenings in the outside world. Reception was usually good. Stations could be picked up from throughout Canada and the United States as well as distant countries of the world.

Especially appreciated was a program originating in Edmonton called *The Northern Messenger*. Each Saturday evening at ten o'clock the card games and reading stopped while everyone listened to messages sent from friends and relatives "outside." Almost every broadcast carried an item or two for someone on the *St. Roch*. "It makes you feel they haven't forgotten about us."

The mail patrol wouldn't be leaving until sometime in March, but on Christmas everyone wrote letters home. Later, Sergeant Anderton made up his year-end report and had Seeley wireless it to Ottawa. In it he stated that the *St. Roch* detachment had traveled 5,201 nautical miles by schooner, and 182 by dog team in four local patrols to places along the coast. He noted that the fur year had been poor in the vicinity and caribou not numerous. The Eskimos, however, had been fairly prosperous, owning schooners and good outfits. With the exception of a few families, all were well educated, speaking and writing English fairly well.

He reported there had been no serious illness, and recommended that Constables Larsen and Foster be promoted to the rank of corporal.

[9]

WITH THE COMING of the new year, each day the twilight that outlined the southern hills at midday grew brighter and lasted longer. One afternoon near the middle of January, sun dogs were seen high over the ship. Glowing spots in the sky caused by light rays shining on ice crystals, sun dogs were considered an omen of bad weather.

A three-day storm blew up that night.

A minute before noon on the eighteenth, a blaze of eye-searing sunlight burned briefly over the hilltops. Its sight brought a cheer from the watching Mounties. In another minute it had vanished, but the elevation of spirits it had brought remained. The next day the entire disc of the sun was visible for twenty minutes. The day after that it was up for nearly an hour.

There was another display of sun dogs, followed by a week of storms. When they ended there were four hours of sunlight so dazzling that no one dared venture out without dark glasses. Snow blindness could easily be suffered by the careless or unwary. Despite its brightness, the sun was still too low to heat the atmosphere appreciably. Men sweated in direct sunlight, but were chilled if they stepped into a shadow. Warm weather was a long time off.

In February a message from Aklavik ordered that a patrol

be sent to Darnley Bay, fifty miles to the east, to hunt for two white trappers who had not been heard from for several months. Anderton and Foster immediately set out. Traveling was poor, the sea ice being extremely rough, and there was deep, soft snow in the mountains. Reaching Darnley Bay, they had to search an unknown district before they found the two trappers in good health and comfortable. Having no reason to communicate with the outside world, they had stayed on their traplines. The patrol covered 198 miles in eight days.

In March, Seeley intercepted a wireless message that Constable Wall of Baillie Island had gone with a native guide to Aklavik to get the winter mail. Ten days later Anderton and Foster prepared to go meet them on their return. One of the men had become increasingly grouchy and cantankerous, complaining about everything and nothing.

"Pack your things," the sergeant told him. "We're taking you to Baillie Island. We'll pick you up next summer."

They reached Baillie after three days' travel over the ice of Franklin Bay, then had to wait three weeks for the return of Wall and his guide. On the way back from Aklavik, they had run into violent storms and had spent most of the time holed up in igloos.

The arrival of the mail was the big event of the year at Langton Bay. Christmas parcels were opened, and letters written nine months before were read, reread, and passed around. Bags of newspapers and magazines had piled up in Edmonton for half a year awaiting transportation. They had come by rail to Fort McMurray, then by dogsled over the frozen waterways of the north.

The days were soon as long as the nights. The sun's warmth was felt again. The canvas covering was stripped off the ship and the wooden framework knocked apart and stowed. Repainting and other outside maintenance work began. The supplies that had been cached ashore were sledded back to the ship. The snowdrifts around the vessel began to melt, and ponds formed on the ice each afternoon refroze glass-hard when the sun went down.

Henry Larsen learned by wireless that he had been promoted to corporal as of April first. Later on in the month Anderton and Foster made a patrol of over two hundred miles. They visited Cape Parry, Letty Harbour, and Bennett Point, all to the north of Langton Bay on the Parry Peninsula.

The sun rose a few minutes after midnight on May 16, not to set again until July 27. Under its continuous circling the surrounding land was soon bare of snow. Torrents of muddy meltwater rushed out of the hills and across the lowlands to cut dirty channels and form murky pools on the sea ice. With the melting of the snow on shore, bright green grass and tiny vivid flowers popped up. Swarms of insects hatched out of the tundra to hover in buzzing clouds over the land. Even on shipboard there were few places safe from the maddening mosquitoes, deerflies, and no-see-um gnats.

By mid-June the floes in Franklin Bay were being cracked apart by winds and currents, but inside the sandpit Langton Bay stayed solid. The ice around the propeller and rudder of the *St. Roch* was cut away, the sails were rerigged, and the engine run and tested. With everything done that could be done to get ready for navigation, the crew spent the dragging time jigging for tomcod and hunting seal.

Early in July the engineers, working underneath the engine, heard water gurgling below. "It won't be long now!"

On the eleventh, ten months and three days after the *St. Roch* arrived at Langton Bay, a strong southeast wind broke up the ice that held her. The engine was started. The anchors were raised. She rounded the spit and caught the current carrying the floes up Franklin Bay to Amundsen Gulf. Stopping at Baillie Island to pick up the man who had been left there in March, she went on to Herschel Island

87

and loaded fuel and supplies. Then, carrying Inspector Eames, who had replaced Vernon Kemp as O.C. Western Arctic, she made a patrol to Bernard Harbour.

The *St. Roch* got back to Herschel on August 21 and left August 26 to winter and refit in Vancouver. She arrived there September 23.

The crew were given leave. Some left for new assignments. In October, Larsen was promoted to sergeant and Foster got his corporal's stripes. "Better late than never."

During refitting, the ship was given a larger deckhouse, which included a wireless room aft of the companionway. The big, unwieldy leg-o'-mutton mainsail was recut to a triangular shape half its original size, and the backstays of the masts were finally rigged. More powerful deck machinery was installed, but a request for a bigger engine was turned down.

On June 27, 1930, the *St. Roch* sailed for the North again with Sergeant Anderton in command and Sergeant Larsen as navigator. Olsen, a corporal now, was first mate, and Kells, chief engineer. Jack Foster had been sent to the Eastern Arctic for duty at Bache Peninsula, Ellesmere Island. Dad Parry was cook, but the rest of the crew was new.

The *St. Roch* was the first ship to reach Herschel Island that year. On August 3, carrying Inspector Eames, she left for Cambridge Bay.

At Baillie Island the inspector held court over a case of child murder. He then closed the detachment because of its poor location on a low sandspit in danger of being awash in heavy gales. The *St. Roch* transferred the constables to Pearce Point, two days' steaming to the east. Provisions and lumber for the new buildings were unloaded, and the ship proceeded on.

A few miles west of Bernard Harbour a small schooner was sighted, hard aground. It was a trader's vessel carrying a quarter million dollars' worth of furs. On the first attempt to pull the craft off, the towrope broke, twisted around the *St. Roch*'s propeller, and left her helpless. The detachment at Bernard Harbour was contacted by radio. A vessel came out and towed the *St. Roch* to the bay, where the propeller could be cleared. The next day the stranded schooner was refloated after two hours of hard tugging.

From there the *St. Roch* went on to the Coppermine River, Coronation Gulf, to pick up a man who had gone insane after suffering from severe exposure the previous winter. Two days later she was at Cambridge Bay. The work there completed, the crew set out for a quick trip back to Herschel Island.

Eight miles away from Cambridge Bay there was a sudden grating. The *St. Roch* shivered to a stop and listed over, hard aground. All night long she bumped and scraped bottom in a heavy swell, and for a time all hands feared she would have to be abandoned. In the morning the cargo was unloaded to the beach two miles away to lighten ship. Two days later the *Baychimo* came along and pulled her off. The remainder of the voyage back to Herschel was without incident, except that the passengers, the constables leaving for the "outside" and the insane man, were constantly seasick.

The *St. Roch* was reprovisioned and left immediately for winter quarters at Tree River on Coronation Gulf, eighty miles east of Coppermine. Compared to most of the coast, it was a pleasant place. High hills protected the harbor. There were lots of fish in the river and an abundance of arctic hares and ptarmigan in the hills to vary the winter menu. The men set nets and caught over three thousand large salmon for dog feed. The ship began freezing in on October 19, and was framed and covered with the canvas.

The routine of the detachment was much like that at Langton Bay two years earlier. There were lots of white foxes in the region, and some of the men ran traplines ashore to catch them.

During the winter the crew overhauled the vessel completely and built a six-ton lightering scow for landing stores at the detachments. Because of the alterations made in Vancouver the previous year, the *St. Roch* was more comfortable in cold weather.

A patrol went out to Bathurst Inlet 190 miles to the east. There Sergeant Anderton learned of the accidental death of an Eskimo, Kamowuak, which had occurred the previous summer. A herd of caribou had been seen near the natives' summer camp. Running out, the Eskimos circled the herd and began firing. When the shooting was over, Kamowuak was found dying from a bullet that had passed through a caribou then struck him.

The *St. Roch* remained in the Arctic continuously until 1934. She spent four consecutive winters at Tree River, supplying the detachments from Herschel Island to Cambridge Bay during open navigation. Larsen, Kells, Farrar, and Parry stayed with the ship. Jack Foster returned from the Eastern Arctic in 1932, and Sergeant Anderton was relieved by Sergeant G. T. Makinson the following year.

Assignments to the crew were for two years unless a man applied to stay on longer. Changes in personnel were made at Herschel on the ship's arrival from winter quarters. The relief men would travel down the Mackenzie to Aklavik, then go by small boat to Herschel Island. Those returning outside would usually catch the last boat from Aklavik. With the passing years, airplanes were seen more frequently in the North, and some men were transported by air.

When it was learned that Captain Gillen had fallen from a ship at Vancouver and been drowned, Dad Parry said, "It must've been the bottle."

"Yah, he was too good a seaman when he was sober to fall overboard."

In 1931 the *Baychimo* lost her annual race with the ice. On the first of October, en route to Point Barrow with a

90

million dollars' worth of fur in her holds, she was caught in the pack. Captain Cornwall decided against wintering aboard and moved the crew to shore, half a mile away, where they built huts. In late November, after a two-day blizzard, the thirteen-hundred-ton ship had vanished. It was concluded that she had been crushed and sank. The following spring the men were rescued and returned to Vancouver.

Reports began coming in of sightings of the vessel hundreds of miles west of Herschel Island. In April of 1932 an Alaskan boarded the ship, saw the furs in the hold, but was unable to salvage them. In August she was seen several times by Eskimos, drifting north. The following year she was again sighted by the crew of a trading schooner. Several attempts to board her failed, and eventually she vanished for good and became another ghost ship.

While at Tree River the *St. Roch* was involved with a murder. Fritz Schurer, who was trapping near Detention Harbour, a few miles east, was shot and killed in December of 1931 by a feebleminded Eskimo woman named Kobvella, with whom he had been living. Learning of the incident, a patrol investigated and returned the body to Tree River. Schurer had died with arms outstretched and frozen in that position. The Mounties had to build an extra-wide coffin to hold the body. It was placed in a nearby warehouse.

In the spring a grave was dug in a small cemetery by building fires and melting the frozen ground. One of the other graves was that of a Mounted Policeman. It was rumored that he had found a famous explorer sick with influenza and had nursed him back to health. When the Mountie in turn had got sick, the explorer had gone on his way and left him to die.

One nice day in May of 1932, after the thaw set in, Anderton said, "I guess we'd better go up and bury Fritz." The grave had filled with water, and the coffin floated. After Dad

91

Parry read the burial service, rocks were piled on the outsized coffin to sink it so that the grave could be filled.

Kobvella was brought to the ship and a hearing held. She said that Schurer had become jealous because she had made clothes for another trapper, Peter Brandt. He had threatened her with a knife, loaded his rifle, and said he was going to kill Brandt. While he was putting on his boots she got hold of the gun and shot him. She was later tried for the crime and taken to Aklavik. After serving a year's sentence, she was sent back to her people on Coronation Gulf.

With the passing years Henry Larsen continued to develop his Arctic knowledge. He took every opportunity to go hunting. On patrols he used every chance to visit the natives and learn their customs and language. His English improved too, and though he never lost his Norwegian accent, he became easy to understand. He studied the currents and weather signs and continued to sharpen his already keen "nose for ice." He depended more on his strong sense of direction than on the magnetic compass, which was inaccurate in the vicinity of the magnetic pole. He relied for navigation on landmarks, prevailing wind and swell directions, and the sun and stars.

When the *St. Roch* was under way, Larsen spent most of his time in the crow's nest. One day, while they were cruising a calm and open sea, Foster came on deck to check the outfall from the bilge pump. Looking up, he called, "How does she look, Skipper?"

"Not a thing in sight, Yack!"

"We'll be in ice in half an hour!" Foster said.

Half an hour later they were in ice. This happened several times, and Larsen demanded to know how an engineer could predict the nearness of ice so accurately.

"Oh, I've got something down below that tells me." Foster took him to the engine room and indicated the thermometers on the engine cooling system. "When we get near ice, the water gets colder and the temperature drops."

Larsen never forgot his hope of taking the *St. Roch* through the Northwest Passage. Every official he met heard his arguments. Detachments in both Eastern and Western Arctic could be supplied in one year by a single ship. In 1928 the Hudson's Bay Company schooner *Fort St. James* had brought supplies to Gjoa Haven from the east by way of Lancaster Sound. "If the *Gjoa* and *St. James* could get through, there's no reason why the *St. Roch* can't."

Dad Parry, besides caring for the medical needs of the crew, was counted on by the natives to doctor their ailments too. A young Eskimo mother with a crying baby came to the ship complaining that she had breast pains and could not feed her child. With warm water and soap he scrubbed away a lifetime's accumulation of encrusted dirt. Milk spurted from the breasts, relieving the pain and silencing the cries of the hungry baby.

During all the years he was among them, Parry never became accustomed to the foul odors of primitives who never bathed or washed their clothing and who favored a diet that would kill most civilized men. Once, invited to repay the visit of a family he had entertained aboard the *St. Roch,* he went ashore to the native camp. When the host held open the tent flap for him to enter, the nauseating smell of half-rotten meat, rancid blubber, and untidy living habits, made him throw up on the spot.

Jack Foster, though, seemed able to adjust to any condition. He spent a lot of time around the villages and, in turn, the ship was often visited by Eskimo girls bringing handmade gifts to him.

The ship returned to Vancouver in the fall of 1934 for a much-needed overhaul. A more powerful engine was again requested and denied. Sergeant Makinson was replaced by Sergeant J. U. Eddy.

While "outside," Henry met Mary Hargreaves, whose father was master of the yacht of a prominent timberman. They were married in December. Parry found a wife that year too, and in June of 1935 their wives were on the pier when they left for the North again.

The *St. Roch* spent that winter at Cambridge Bay. While he was there, Larsen learned by wireless that he was father of a daughter who was named Doreen. He never saw her as a baby because the next winter the ship remained at Cambridge Bay too.

In August of 1937, while in the company of the *St. Roch,* the *Fort St. James* was caught in an ice squeeze in Dolphin and Union Strait. The Hudson's Bay supply schooner was crushed and went down with everything, including her captain's false teeth. The twelve persons aboard were rescued by the police vessel, which was only seventy feet away at the time. Though she took a terrific beating from the pack, the stout hull of the *St. Roch* withstood the pressure and she worked free.

Also in 1937, the Hudson's Bay Company's schooner *Aklavik* navigated Bellot Strait, a narrow channel separating Boothia Peninsula from Somerset Island. She exchanged freight with the icebreaker *Nascopie* at Fort Ross. The hazardous waterway between Franklin Strait and the Gulf of Boothia had five times defeated the *Fox* in 1858–1859 during M'Clintock's search for the Franklin expedition. Technically, the meeting of the *Nascopie* and the *Aklavik* was a completion of the Northwest Passage. But no single vessel had yet succeeded in making a west-to-east voyage through the passage.

When he returned to Vancouver in 1937, Larsen met his two-year-old daughter for the first time. The fair-haired little girl was less interested in the stranger in Mounted Police uniform who her mother said was "Daddy" than in the big black husky he had brought home.

Jack Foster, who had not gone north on the previous cruise, rejoined in 1937. He was married now too, having wed Siddie Cornwell, whom he had known since she was thirteen years old. Tall and slim, with dark eyes and hair, she was a stepdaughter of "Jockey" Jones, the R.C.M.P. riding instructor who put on the Musical Ride for many years. Siddie had her Irish stepfather's sense of humor and her English mother's beauty. "You might have known," the envious said, "that old Calico Jack would land the prettiest girl in British Columbia."

When the *St. Roch* left for the Arctic in 1938, Henry Larsen was in charge of police duties as well as navigation. Wintering once more at Cambridge Bay, they returned to the Naval dockyard at Esquimalt, British Columbia, in 1939. Larsen moved his family to Victoria, close by. He had a son now, Gordon, born in 1938.

The Second World War broke out in September. Canada mobilized, and the Force was drained of men. Ships, airplanes, and pilots left the North for war duty, and supplying of the Arctic detachments became a serious problem. Commissioner S. T. Wood, whose idea the *St. Roch* originally had been, ordered Sergeant Larsen to determine whether it was feasible to supply the Western and Eastern Arctic subdivisions in one year with a single ship. His instructions were to sail the next year from Vancouver to Halifax by way of the Northwest Passage.

[10]

EAGER TO PROVE HIS POINT at last, Henry Larsen went East early in 1940 to order equipment and supplies for the *St. Roch*. At Windsor, Ontario, a car was assigned to carry him around. The driver was a husky, blond young constable from Calgary, John Friederich. Larsen told Friederich about the ship, what they had been doing in the North, and of the proposed Northwest Passage voyage. Friederich, who didn't care for the East, had two years yet to serve of a five-year enlistment. He said he would like to go on the expedition too. Larsen liked the man's looks and arranged for his transfer to the ship as second engineer.

The key members of the crew all had long service on the *St. Roch*. Foster was chief engineer, Farrar, first mate, and Parry, cook. A. J. Chartrand and J. M. Monette were inexperienced seamen. Constable P. G. Hunt, on transfer to Coppermine, was a temporary crewman. Special Constable E. C. Hadley would be wireless operator.

All the machinery was overhauled at the Naval dockyard. Once again Foster begged for a more powerful engine to be installed, but he was turned down.

"There's a war on, you know."

The ship was dry-docked and the hull examined. Even after its years of rugged Arctic service, it was in fine condition. The crew did all the cleaning, scraping, and painting.

The families of Larsen, Foster, and Parry were living in Victoria and came to know one another well. Mary Larsen and Siddie Foster were close friends. They leaned on each other when their husbands, not used to living with women, became difficult to handle. Sometimes the children made Henry nervous. Strong-willed and accustomed to being in complete command, he would stalk out of the house and go to the Fosters' in search of a sympathetic ear. One day Mary called to tell Siddie he was coming. "Don't feed him. He'll come home when he's hungry."

Siddie made him a cup of tea, talked to him like a mother, and he did go home when he was hungry.

The early months of 1940 quickly passed, and on the ninth of June the *St. Roch* left for Vancouver. Of the days that followed, Larsen later wrote: "After having loaded our little vessel to full capacity with fuel and provisions for our own need, and also for our Western Arctic Detachments, we left Vancouver at 2:50 a.m. June 23rd, 1940, and proceeded northward through the Inside Passage as far as the north end of Vancouver Island. From this point we headed 'St. Roch's' blunt bow westward across the Pacific direct from Unimak Pass.

"Some bad weather was encountered, and at times our heavily laden vessel was almost completely submerged, causing large volumes of water to pour into our living quarters, adding discomfort to the members who were off watch trying to get a little sleep. This is a hard thing to do when one constantly is on the verge of being tossed out of one's bunk with each roll of the ship. Sometimes the galley fire had to be put out owing to the backdraft, caused by the quick rolling motion of the ship, blowing down the smokestack. Some of our boys had never before been on a vessel or salt water, but to their everlasting credit they stood up well; and taking everything as a matter of fact, they soon found their sea legs.

"On July 4th we passed through Unimak Pass from the

Pacific into the Bering Sea. We took shelter for a while in Akun Cove in order to tidy the ship up a bit before proceeding to Dutch Harbour. Here we took the opportunity to catch a few cod and halibut and had a good feed, which we all needed. On July 6th we arrived in Dutch Harbour. Next day being Sunday, we were royally entertained by the officers and crew of the U. S. Coast Guard Cutter 'Shoshone' of the Bering Sea Patrol. Some of them were, I think, a bit amused at seeing our small vessel whose decks were completely hidden under hundreds of coal sacks, oil drums, and small rowboats, stacks of cases containing fresh potatoes, eggs and various vegetables that we couldn't store in our holds, and on top of all this deadload were, of course, our men in our Mounted Police uniforms, trying to act and walk in a dignified and military manner as laid down in our training.

"However, friendly relations were soon established between our men and the American sailors who began to swarm aboard the 'St. Roch,' and to entertain us with tales that they had heard or read about in the States, regarding some of the exploits of the R.C.M. Police. Some of the feats they mentioned, I believed, far surpassed those accomplished by Superman or Flash Gordon; anyway they were all fine boys, and we soon had enough volunteers to man ten ships like the 'St. Roch.' "

That night, while returning from the hearty celebration aboard the American vessel, Frenchy Chartrand walked off the pier. The tide was out and he landed standing upright in the mud. Unable to free himself, he would have been drowned by the returning tide had not two shipmates come along shortly afterward and heard his cries for help.

They left Dutch Harbor on the ninth. The weather was foul all the way to Teller. Good omens seen on the Pacific crossing were replaced by increasingly bad ones. The voyage was the stormiest that Larsen had ever experienced on the Bering Sea. Wireless reports from ships and land stations farther on indicated bad ice and weather conditions all

The St. Roch *under construction, Vancouver, 1928*

The broad-beamed wooden schooner right after launching

As the sea froze, the rounded hull prevented stoving in

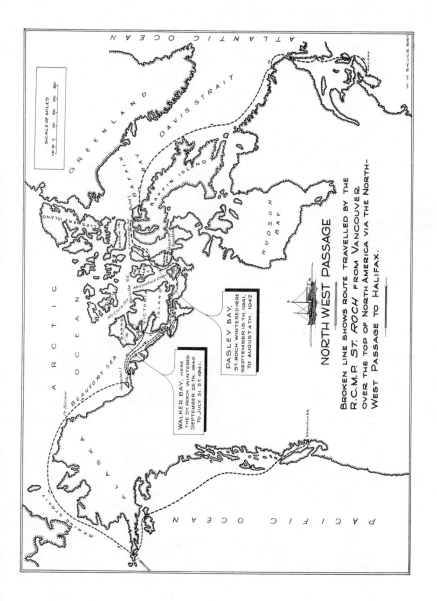

NORTH WEST PASSAGE

Broken line shows route travelled by the
R.C.M.P. ST. ROCH from Vancouver,
over the top of North America via the North-
West Passage to Halifax.

WALKER BAY, HERE
THE ST. ROCH WINTERED
SEPTEMBER 25TH, 1940
TO JULY 31, ST. 1941.

PASLEY BAY,
ST. ROCH WINTERED HERE
SEPTEMBER 15TH, 1941,
TO AUGUST 4TH. 1942

SCALE OF MILES
100 50 0 100 200 300 400

ATLANTIC OCEAN

GREENLAND

DAVIS STRAIT

BAFFIN BAY

BAFFIN ISLAND

HUDSON BAY

ARCTIC OCEAN

BEAUFORT SEA

ALASKA

BERING STRAIT

PACIFIC OCEAN

VANCOUVER

Iced in, the Mounties proceeded by dogsled

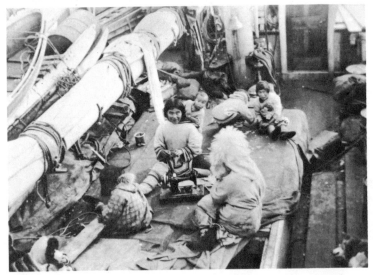

The Eskimo guide's family and dogs camped on the hatch

The Norse navigator was made a R.C.M.P. inspector in 1946

*The triumphant St. Roch sails into the narrows at Vancouver,
escorted by two police cruisers*

*Showing her colors, the St. Roch completes her voyage
circling the North American continent*

The Governor General of Canada honors Superintendent Larsen, R.C.M.P., in 1960

through the Arctic. The *St. Roch* reached Teller on the fifteenth and loaded half a ton of dog feed. In the little town the wounds of the Amundsen-Nobile feud seemed to have been healed.

The *St. Roch* reached Point Barrow on July 22. The crew went ashore for a brief visit, but because of the dangerous, ice-threatened anchorage, they didn't stay long. East of Barrow the ice was bad, with fog and northerly winds that kept the pack in against the coast. The *St. Roch* was constantly getting beset.

One day when the fog had lifted briefly, Larsen was in the crow's nest, watching for leads and calling down orders to Farrar, who was at the wheel. Farrar, in turn, would pass the engine orders on to Friederich, on watch in the engine room. Besides carrying out his duties, the second engineer was trying to read a book. With each clang of the bell he would lay aside his reading, work the throttle, and crank the handwheel that operated the reverse gear.

The vessel was in a delicate situation, the signals were coming fast, and Friederich's book was getting interesting. In the confusion, he missed a bell and did the opposite of what was called for. The ship took a neck-snapping jolt from a floe that Larsen had been trying to avoid.

The skipper came roaring down the rigging and began to chew out Farrar for misinterpreting his orders. After a loud exchange of words, both headed below.

Friederich heard them coming, Larsen growling in his Norwegian accent and the mate, an Englishman with a Liverpudlian dialect, saying, "I can speak the king's English —it's just that that stupid German down there can't understand it!"

The book had vanished when they got there.

Not only Larsen and Farrar, but every man on the ship had an accent, depending on his background. The crew of the *St. Roch* was a true cross section of Canada's many ethnic groups and regions. Those from the West had their own manner of speaking, as did Foster from New Brunswick and Parry, the Welshman. Chartrand's accent was the thickest. A French-Canadian, he spoke English poorly. In spite of it, he was popular with his shipmates. Possessed of a good sense of humor and a love for work, "Frenchy" was a handsome fellow with dark, swarthy skin and black, curly hair.

Monette still hadn't conquered seasickness. Any ship movement made him ill, and the rough passage through the pack didn't help. "I hope I get over it. I sure want to make this trip."

Dad Parry, too, still had trouble when it was rough, but carried on. As on previous cruises, besides being cook he doctored the injured, nursed the sick, and did the dirty jobs no one else cared to do.

The *St. Roch* made poor progress until she reached Cross Island on August 10. Fog had begun freezing to the rigging and young ice was forming around the vessel. Then the wind calmed, visibility cleared, and the pressure began to ease. The crew began blasting with ice bombs, and by early afternoon the *St. Roch* was proceeding eastward in a good lead. A northeast wind sprang up and helped clear the ice.

The ship reached Herschel Island on August 12 and was met by Inspector Bullard in the R.C.M.P. boat *Aklavik*. He had come from Aklavik to receive the coal and supplies brought from Vancouver. The village at Herschel was abandoned. The natives who had survived the 1928 epidemic had moved to the Mackenzie delta when the Hudson's Bay Company changed the location of its trading post to Tuktoyaktuk, commonly known as Tuk Tuk.

Some of the drums of diesel oil unloaded on the first trip to the Arctic in 1928 were brought back aboard and stowed on deck. The two vessels were stormbound until the eighteenth. At noon the weather began to moderate and at half past three they got under way for Tuk Tuk, east of the Mackenzie. The wind was calm, and there was fog and a heavy swell on the Beaufort Sea. The sounding line was kept going through the night, and the cry of the leadsman was as constant as the throb of the diesel engine. "Mark ten, no bottom!"

The *St. Roch* anchored on August 21 at Tuktoyaktuk, where cargo was transferred to the *Aklavik*. In the morning coal was discharged, dried fish and other supplies taken on, and the ship readied for sea. The fuel tanks were refilled from the barrels picked up at Herschel Island. The weather had turned fine and clear. The Mounties were anxious to sail, but they had to wait for Constable George Peters to arrive from Aklavik.

Peters had become engaged to a nurse at the hospital there. Her assignment completed, she had returned to her home in Halifax. He was anxious to join her so that they could be married, but he still had some time to spend in the North. Hearing about the projected voyage of the *St. Roch* through the Northwest Passage, he decided that if he could be assigned to the ship he would get outside the same year. A qualified engineer, he contacted the vessel by radio and proposed that he and Friederich trade jobs. John didn't care one way or the other and agreed to the change.

Peters arrived on August 23, and Inspector Bullard and Friederich left the ship. A sick native woman and her child and two boys from the Anglican school were taken aboard to go to Cambridge Bay. The *St. Roch* sailed from Tuk Tuk shortly after noon, towing a motorboat. She headed eastward into thick fog as soundings were taken. "Mark seven! Deep eight!"

After stopping briefly at Bernard Harbour to check a gasoline cache and to land coal and dried fish, they proceeded on to Coppermine. Because Monette was still suffering from seasickness, he was transferred to shore duty and Constable Hunt remained in his place. Three dogs were taken aboard.

The *St. Roch* left Coppermine on the morning of September 2 in clear weather. The crew was hopeful of making up some of the time lost due to bad ice and fog. In years past the ship usually got to Cambridge Bay about the middle of August. Since it was still several days' cruising from there, the skipper was concerned about getting through the Northwest Passage this season. But he wouldn't commit himself. "Let's hope this weather holds."

The weather held, but the engine began running rough. Foster said they would have to stop and clean the fuel valves. Twelve hours after they left Coppermine, the anchor was dropped at Tree River. While the valves were being cleaned, fresh water was taken from a creek. They had planned to get away that evening, but the motorboat ran aground off the mouth of the creek while carrying water. She couldn't be pulled off because of the falling tide. "Now we've got to wait until high water tomorrow afternoon."

Using the smaller boats, the men resumed filling tanks in the morning. The boat was refloated in midafternoon. They kept transporting water until the tanks were full. The *St. Roch* got under way at three fifteen on the morning of the fourth.

The weather was still calm and clear. They made fine time for a few hours, until the engine began acting up. They drifted while the valves were cleaned again, then continued on. Half an hour later they had to stop once more and clean them.

Larsen began to fret. "For once we've got good weather and a chance to make good time. What's the matter anyway, Yack?"

"It's that old oil we picked up at Herschel, Skipper. I think the barrels rusted inside. Looks like that's what's plugging up our valves—little bits of rust too fine to be filtered out."

"Don't put any more of it in the tanks. We've lost too much time already without having to stop and clean valves."

"We put all the old oil in the tanks at Tuk Tuk. It'll just have to work it's way through."

Cape Barrow was abeam at noon. At five thirty the ship was anchored at Wilmot Island to clean valves again. The weather was dark and threatening. In the night a fog moved in, and there was no visibility in the morning. During the day a northeast wind blew the fog away but made the sea too rough for sailing. The ship was moved inside the harbor for better shelter and both anchors put out to hold her. The storm kept her there for two days.

On the seventh the wind dropped, the sea calmed, and they went on to Cambridge Bay, arriving the next morning. The crew worked two twelve-hour days unloading and preparing for sea. When they finished on the tenth a strong easterly was blowing.

That evening Sergeant Larsen spent some time with Hadley in the wireless room exchanging messages with stations to the eastward. A card game was going when he returned to the saloon. "Find out anything, Skipper?"

"If we'd gotten here two weeks ago, we could have made it through all right. The people at Fort Ross say the sea to the north is still open east of Somerset Island, but the pack is in at Gjoa Haven."

"Are we stuck here for the winter, then?" Peters asked.

"We're going back to Amundsen Gulf and see how things look up in Prince of Wales Strait."

"What if we can't get through there?"

"Then we'll winter at Banks Land or Victoria Land."

"Do you think there's a chance of getting through Prince of Wales Strait this late?"

"We won't know till we get there. We're three weeks behind schedule already, so it doesn't look good."

Peters' face was glum.

"Sweeten the pot, George," Foster said, dealing the cards. "Get your mind off your girl. You won't have a wife this year."

[11]

HER WORK COMPLETED at Cambridge Bay, the *St. Roch* got under way for Coppermine on September 10 in the face of threatening weather. Besides her crew she carried a part-Eskimo guide, George Porter, and his family. They lived in a tent set up on the lightering scow carried amidships. Steaming west until nearly dark, the ship anchored for the night. When it was light enough to see in the morning she proceeded on through Dease Strait.

Unable to make headway against a northwest gale, she returned to the lee of Finlayson Island and lay at anchor until the twelfth. An hour after putting to sea again she was turned back by a cold, wet fog. The crew was uneasy. "At this rate we won't even make Amundsen Gulf."

"Then we'll winter at Tree River," Larsen said.

Visibility improved later in the day, and they steamed on until stopped by darkness off the Kent Peninsula. At daybreak of the thirteenth it was misty, but the *St. Roch* crept slowly on through Coronation Gulf, dropping anchor at Tree River in the evening. A southeasterly was blowing. The weather was forbidding.

Gales and heavy rains kept the ship at her old wintering place for two days. She didn't get to Coppermine until the sixteenth. A mail plane was expected so they waited. The time was spent fishing and preparing for winter quarters.

112

The rest of the dogs and gear were taken aboard.

The mail plane arrived the afternoon of the eighteenth and they sailed from Coppermine early on the nineteenth. The weather had turned clear and calm. The ship made excellent progress through Dolphin and Union Strait. Cape Krusenstern was abeam at eleven fifteen. Where the *Fort St. James* had gone down three years before, there was no sign of the pack. "I never saw so little ice here for this time of year," the skipper said.

Peters was smiling again.

"Don't get your hopes up, George. A north wind will stop us dead."

No one whistled on the vessel.

At three thirty she was off Barnard Harbour. By eight she had passed Cape Hope. Amundsen Gulf was ahead. The weather was still favorable, and the *St. Roch* steamed north all night. When the watch changed at four A.M. a fresh northwester was blowing. At eight the wind strengthened and there was no visibility. It cleared at noon and Holman Island was sighted. A few hours later the anchor was dropped off the Hudson's Bay post there.

Larsen had intended to go on to Walker Bay in the morning, but the fog was thick, so they remained at anchor. In the afternoon instructions were received from Aklavik to go to Banks Island and investigate the possibilities of wintering there.

Late in the day the weather cleared, and they left Holman Island. After steaming northwest through a cloudy night, on Sunday morning, September 22, the *St. Roch* came to anchor inside a sandspit at DeSalis Bay. In the afternoon Larsen and Farrar, Peters and Chartrand left in a motorboat to reconnoiter the harbor.

"That spit would protect us from easterlies," Farrar said.

Larsen indicated mounds of rock and gravel on the shore. "That stuff got pushed there by ice being shoved ashore. I'm afraid we'd get too much pressure from the pack here

113

during breakup." The wind began to pick up. "Let's go back to the ship. We'll look around some more tomorrow."

An easterly gale and snow kept them aboard the next day, but on Tuesday they examined the bay further. Larsen wasn't satisfied with what he saw. They searched the surrounding country for a source of fresh water, but the nearest lake was six miles inland.

"That's too far. We can't stay here—everything is against us."

The charts indicated a harbor at Cape Kellett, 150 miles away on the west coast of the island. A local native was questioned about it. He said it was not large enough to accommodate the *St. Roch* safely.

In the hazy dawn of a cold and windy September 25, the *St. Roch* left for Victoria Island, 75 miles to the east. As they crossed the gray, choppy Strait of Prince of Wales, everyone's attention was directed to the north. There was no sign of the pack.

The log entries for the day ended with: "7:45 p.m., arrived and anchored at winter cove, Walker Bay, three fathoms water, thirty fathoms cable, wind westerly, freshening with dark cloudy weather. Night watches maintained.

"Thursday, September 26.—At winter cove, strong N.W. wind, overcast with fog. Commenced to fill fuel oil tanks from drums on deck. Anchorage considered unsafe for wintering owing to shallow water; proceeded to S.E. portion of Walker Bay, anchored in small cove, laying north and south. Good swinging room. Anchored in ten fathoms of water."

The ending days of September and the beginning of October were filled with backbreaking work. The men moved sacks of coal, empty oil drums, and nonfreezable stores to the beach. The dogs were installed ashore, and fishnets and a seal net set for feed for them. When the weather was too severe for outside duties, stores were sorted in the hold and the bosun's locker cleaned and rearranged.

There was plenty of time for such inside work. Rain, snow, sleet, and gales came from all around the compass. The Arctic delivered everything but an ice pack.

"Friday, October 4.—Vessel in winter quarters. Crew employed throughout the day hauling fresh water from lake to ship. Strong easterly wind. 6:00 p.m., steamed into position and dropped starboard anchor. Watches maintained."

And on the fifth: "Crew employed hauling out scow on beach, also drying and stowing away sails and gear in hold for the winter. Light easterly wind. Weather turning cold, freezing around beach."

As in other years, canned goods were moved from the unheated hold to cupboards and lockers in the living quarters, and the pipes were disconnected and drained. The drums for melting ice for water were set up in saloon and forecastle. The morning of the fourteenth dawned calm and clear, and the ship was surrounded by young ice that had formed in the night. But in the afternoon an east wind rose, broke up the ice and blew it away to the west.

The lake on shore froze sufficiently for the cutting of the winter's fresh water supply. While some of the men cut the blocks, others set fishnets under the ice for trout. Hunters went out for game to feed themselves and the dogs.

On the afternoon of October 21 the *St. Roch* moved to the lower end of the bay for more shelter from an easterly so wild that both anchors had to be dropped. Blowing spray glazed the ship's sides and icicles, pointing away from the wind, festooned the rigging. When it calmed the crew began the erection of the framework for the canvas housing. Young ice formed around the ship again. When it was three inches thick, the weather turned mild, and the new ice got soft and mushy. Then it started snowing.

"By golly, I never saw such crazy weather in all my life," Larsen said.

It stayed mild with variable winds for five days, with the ice too soft to walk upon. Then, the morning of the thirtieth, the wind changed to north-northwest, the temperature dropped abruptly. The ice hardened and thickened. Cracking and crushing it before her, the *St. Roch* was moved into position for wintering and anchored in ten fathoms three hundred yards from the beach. The next day she was frozen in solid, and the entire bay was sheathed in ice. Outside, driven by the norther and pressed southward by the freezing polar ice cap, the pack came marching down and jammed the Strait of Prince of Wales.

On October 31, Henry Larsen entered in his log: "This has been one of the latest freezeups on record owing to prevailing easterly winds which caused young ice moving offshore as fast as forming. End of navigation season, 1940. Total mileage for season, 5,240 miles."

Playing cards that evening in the saloon and listening to the creaking of the vessel's timbers as the freezing sea pressed against her, he said, "If I could have known the freeze-up would be this late, we might be in Halifax right now."

"But we're not," Parry said, pouring coffee all around. "One nice thing about a late freeze, we have only nine months to wait for the breakup."

"*Only* nine months!" Peters snorted. "I didn't know when I was lucky."

Routine aboard the *St. Roch* was little different than in previous winters. When weather permitted, the men hunted and trapped and made short patrols to explore the countryside, getting men and dogs in condition for the long expeditions planned for the return of sun. Since they were much farther north at Walker Bay than at any of the previous winter quarters, they last saw the sun for the year on November 16. This was nine days earlier than at Cambridge Bay and twenty-two days sooner than at Tree River. It would not reappear until January 26.

Whereas in other years cardplaying had been the principal means of passing idle hours, because of the war listening to the radio now occupied more time. When newscasts were on everything stopped, and the crew gathered around to listen to the happenings in Europe. The varied backgrounds of the men made it possible for at least one person aboard to understand most languages that came over the air. Chartrand could translate from Radio Paris, and occasionally Larsen would hear broadcasts from Oslo in Norwegian. At this stage of hostilities little of the news was good. The gloating English-language transmissions from Berlin were infuriating. "It's a good thing old Hitler can't hear what you boys are saying about him," Parry said, "or he'd send some Heinkels over here."

Some of the younger men were impatient to get at the enemy. They felt their Northern service was cheating them of a chance to join the other Mounties who had taken leave to enter the Canadian forces. News of bombings of cities by the Luftwaffe fired their patriotism. "It makes you feel so helpless sitting up here doing nothing!"

"You're doing a job somebody has to do."

"But the war might be over before we get back."

"The way the news has been it'll be going on for a long time."

In the First War, Parry had seen duty in the trenches. "You're not missing a thing not being over there, Lad. It gets mighty boring here, but at least we're not being shot at."

"Who's scared of being shot at?"

"You've never been under fire or you wouldn't be so anxious."

They never missed a broadcast of *The Northern Messenger* on Saturday evenings. Messages could now be sent from the ship to a receiving station in Churchill, Manitoba, and retransmitted over land lines to the outside. And through *The Messenger*, familiar voices were heard aboard the *St. Roch*. Brief, one-minute greetings could be telephoned to the station and rebroadcast.

117

Back home, families were carrying on as usual. In Victoria, Mary Larsen and Mrs. Parry were busy with their children. Siddie Foster had returned to Vancouver, where she was operating a beauty parlor. She spent some of her free time knitting for the Red Cross and helping with a group of old-age pensioners. She was invited to join the Women's Division of the Royal Canadian Air Force, but declined.

Siddie's services as a hairdresser would have been welcome on the *St. Roch*. Dad Parry was a fair hand with the clippers, but the crew generally looked shaggy. Some, including Jack, let their beards grow. He never cut his whiskers during the cold months in the Arctic, but kept his upper lip clean-shaven to prevent his exhaled breath from freezing to a moustache. In their skin clothing, the unshaven men bore no resemblance to the classic neat, trim Mountie.

Frenchy Chartrand, though, always looked as if he had just stepped out of the bandbox. His shipmates called him the best-dressed man in the Arctic. He had had his deerskin clothing especially tailored by an Eskimo seamstress. Parka, pants, and mukluks were ornamented with designs made of alternating strips and squares of light and dark skin. He was a chesty fellow six feet tall, and he liked to go around in the coldest weather stripped to the waist. Some thought he was the toughest man in the Arctic too, or else the craziest.

No major patrols were carried out until after the new year, when the days brightened with the approach of the returning sun. On January 20, 1941, Chartrand, Peters, and the guide, George Porter, left for Holman Island to pick up the mail and interview natives. The sun came back on the twenty-sixth, but they didn't see it because of a heavy overcast. During the 195-mile patrol, bad weather kept them in camp for days at a time. They did not return until the eleventh of February.

On February 4, Larsen and John Kudlao, a local native,

made a five-day trip to Ramsay Island, some miles to the northwest. The purpose of the patrol was to observe ice conditions in Prince of Wales Strait, to find the best route for a trip to Banks Land. There were open leads southwest of the island and heavy pressure ridges against the shore ice. To the northwest there was no open water, but the ice was very rough.

At Holman Island, Chartrand and Peters had been told that an airplane was expected at Coppermine on March 15. Having mail to send out, Sergeant Larsen left on February 23 with Porter and nine police dogs to go to Holman Island. Traveling was good. They covered the seventy-five miles in two days. Constable Monette, who had had to leave the *St. Roch* because of seasickness, arrived with mail on the twenty-eighth. Larsen and Porter started back for Walker Bay in the morning and reached the ship the next evening.

The Banks Land Patrol left the *St. Roch* on March 17. Leaving Corporal Foster in charge of the detachment, Larsen, Peters, and Porter set out with two eighteen-foot komatiks, each carrying a ton of supplies and equipment. One sled was pulled by seven dogs, the other by eight. Orders were to investigate rumors of violations of the Northwest Territories Game Act, to register firearms, and to interview a Mrs. Wolki concerning the estate of her late husband.

The sleds had little difficulty crossing Prince of Wales Strait, but as they followed the Banks Island coast southward outside the pressure ridge, rough ice kept breaking the mud from the runners. Sand and gravel blown from the dreary, barren land made it hard for the small teams to drag the heavy sleds over the gritty ice. At DeSalis Bay the ice was pushed up against the spit and showed signs of having broken up and refrozen several times during the winter. "It's a good job we didn't winter here," Peters said. "Our goose would have been cooked when that ice was milling around."

Traveling overland to Sachs Harbour was even more difficult. Part of the way was through steep hills, following a crooked, rocky river that was hard for the long and heavy komatiks to negotiate. If they made twenty miles in ten hours, they were lucky. White and blue foxes and countless rabbits showed no fear of man or dogs and hardly moved when the teams approached.

It took seven days to reach the west coast of Banks Island, seventy-five miles from DeSalis Bay. The Arctic Ocean shore was all steep cliffs with little beach. The snow was deep and sugary. In places wet ice, recently frozen, was encountered. Teams, sleds, and men constantly fell into snow-covered tide cracks. In one fall a lead dog injured a front leg and was taken out of harness. The remaining sixty miles to Sachs Harbour required three days.

Five families had their main camp there, and three schooners were pulled out on the shore. The weary Mounties accepted an invitation to stay with Fred Carpenter, a trader, and his family. He was the son of an American whaler father and a Canadian Eskimo mother. The natives, from the Mackenzie River delta, were intelligent and fairly prosperous.

The patrol took life easy the next day or two, cooking dog feed, drying clothing, and repairing equipment. The firearms were registered and inquiries made about Banks Land. On April 3, using Carpenter's toboggan and the best nine of the dogs, Larsen and Porter left for Storkerson Bay, sixty-five miles to the north, to visit the natives there. They got back to Sachs Harbour on the eighth.

For the next few days they attended to various duties. Mrs. Wolki's affairs were settled, and infractions of the law investigated. Larsen and Peters went to open water with hunters and took two seals. Preparations were begun for the return to Walker Bay. The weather was calm and clear, and the bright sun of the lengthening days made the snow disappear quickly from the land.

April 13 was Easter Day. Everyone went to Carpenter's

house for dinner and an Easter celebration. The trader showed movies he had taken, projected from equipment operated by a six-volt battery.

The patrol left Sachs Harbour Monday afternoon. Because of thawing, the return was even more difficult and wearing on men and dogs than the outbound journey. They were stormbound in igloos for days at a time. Once the snowhouse blew down, and they had to build another in a howling gale. The canvas sled covers were put over the new house and lashed down. In spite of the storm, the weather was mild and the house was wet and dripping inside.

The wind calmed and they set out again. After they had gone a mile, the storm returned violently. They went back to the campsite and built another house. In his diary for the day, Larsen wrote: "Sand and gravel blowing down from the land. Skins and equipment wet from snow. Camp dripping and miserable. Mileage, two."

The next day the skies cleared and the wind calmed. They set out again. With the warming weather, Larsen was fearful of a breakup in the sea ice that would prevent their crossing Prince of Wales Strait. They followed the Banks Island coast for a time, then turned gradually eastward on a circling course to avoid the rough ice on the strait. They traveled all night and didn't stop until they were across. After camping at Berkeley Point until noon, they went on.

In midafternoon the crow's nest at the top of the *St. Roch*'s mainmast showed above the horizon. Too tired to hurry, they plodded toward it. Alerted by a lookout, the whole detachment came out to meet the incoming patrol.

"Good to see you back, Skipper," Foster said. "How did it go?"

Larsen brushed the shaggy forty-one days' growth of moustache and beard away from his mouth and scratched an itchy spot on his unbathed skin. "Not bad, considering everything."

The next day, bathed, shaved, and barbered, he completed his report of the patrol to Banks Land: "Sunday, April 27th. Arrived at ship 8:00 p.m. with all members, dogs and equipment in good condition. Total mileage, 592." Thus was recorded one of the toughest patrols in R.C.M.P. history.

Two more short patrols went out before the imminent breakup made traveling over the ice too difficult and dangerous for further sledding. Hunt and Porter left for Holman Island on May 10. They were gone five days, compiling game returns and registering the guns of natives. On the seventeenth, Larsen and Chartrand went north to examine ice conditions and look for anchorages in Prince of Wales Strait preparatory to continuing the Northwest Passage voyage. With the sun always in the sky now, melting snow and rotten ice made travel difficult. They were kept in camp several days by storms and finally reached Princess Royal Island on the twenty-fifth.

On the highest point of the island they found the cache that Captain Robert M'Clure had left while searching for the Franklin expedition. In the *Investigator,* he had entered the Arctic from the west through Bering Strait in 1850. Two years later, caught in the ice north of Banks Land, he abandoned the ship. Trudging eastward five hundred miles to Dealey Island, M'Clure and his crew were rescued in 1853 by Captain Kellett in the *Resolute,* another vessel looking for Sir John. Larsen and Chartrand found the contents of the cache had long been removed.

From Princess Royal they could see a smaller island half a mile away, with open water and a strong current in between. Larsen was encouraged. "We might get an early breakup after all."

Starting back for Walker Bay, they crossed the strait to look for harbors on Banks Land, but found none. Although three of the dogs were sick, they made thirty-five miles in one day. On May 31 they reached Berkeley Point. The ice ahead was covered with water, but they crossed safely and camped with George Porter, who was hunting seal. The next day Larsen returned alone to the ship, leaving Chartrand to help with the seal hunt.

Since all signs promised an early breakup, the *St. Roch* was readied for sea. While the Walker Bay ice was still solid, the men sledded the supplies, fuel, and equipment that had been stored ashore back to the ship and stowed them. They rigged sails and tested the engine.

By the end of June the surrounding land was free of snow, there was open water in Prince of Wales Strait, and the pack was streaming through. Walker Bay broke up early in July, but a prevailing wind from the west kept the entrance jammed with floes.

"We'd better start trying to get out," Larsen said. "I don't want to spend another winter here." On the morning of the thirty-first he alerted the engine room. "Get the enyine going. There's a lead opening in the bay."

Twenty minutes later the *St. Roch* was steaming into the lead through scattered ice. The crew was elated by the throb of the engine, the vibration of the deck, and the lifting of the ship to the gentle swell. Two hours later at Pemmican Point the lead closed and they were stopped. While the *St. Roch* was moored to a floe to await improvement in conditions, the water tanks were filled from pools on the ice. Larsen went to the masthead to watch and wait.

Coming on deck for fresh air, Foster looked up. "Does it look like we can get through Prince of Wales?"

"It's open as far as I can see. Once we get out of here we'll go till we get stopped!"

At one o'clock a lead began opening to the southwest. They were just entering it when Hadley came from the wireless room. "I just got a message from Holman Island that a native boy has been shot. We're to get there as soon as we can and take him to Tuk Tuk."

[12]

JACK GOOSE HAD BEEN accidentally shot through both cheeks by his brother. Frightened and suffering, the ten-year-old was brought aboard early on the morning of August 1 and put in a bunk in the after living quarters under the care of Dad Parry. The *St. Roch* sailed at once for Tuktoyaktuk.

Cruising slowly through thick wet fog past heavy floes a few hours later, Farrar said, "We might have been halfway to Melville Sound by now if this hadn't happened, eh, Skipper?"

"And we might have been beset again, too." Through the mist Larsen watched the endless passing of the pack. "This doesn't look good. There should be hardly any ice in Amundsen Gulf now."

"I hope it doesn't take too long to get to Tuk Tuk and back up to the strait. We can't get to Halifax too soon for me."

"We'll get there when we get there."

Despite adverse winds and bad visibility the ship made good time, and by midnight of August 3 was nearing Tuktoyaktuk. As she inched through fog and wallowed in a swell with a strong northeast wind behind her, the water abruptly shallowed and the keel began to bump the bottom. She was brought about and headed for deeper water. Just holding her own against the gale, she grounded several more times before she was off the shoals.

Until now the wounded Eskimo boy had maintained his native stoicism, but when the rolling ship began to pound bottom he gave in to fear and cried. Parry held him in his arms and comforted him until he fell asleep. Tucking him in, he said, "Poor little kid. He's a brave one."

In late afternoon as the weather improved, they entered the harbor and anchored. Jack Goose was sent ashore to be taken on to Aklavik. Inspector Bullard, O.C. Western Arctic, came aboard with new orders for the *St. Roch*. She would not continue the voyage by way of Prince of Wales Strait. Instead, because of lack of other transport, she would take supplies to the detachments to the east. From Cambridge Bay she would attempt to reach Halifax by way of M'Clintock Channel or Franklin Strait.

Loading fuel and cargo took two days. John Friederich, who had wintered at Arctic Red River on the Mackenzie, rejoined temporarily on transfer to Cambridge Bay. Two native boys were returning home from the Anglican Mission School at Aklavik. The *St. Roch* left Tuk Tuk on August 8. Thick fog and ice made progress slow, and not until the twelfth did she reach Cape Krusenstern, five hundred miles east. One boy was landed, and the ship went on to Coppermine, arriving late that evening. The other boy went ashore, the supplies were unloaded, and she sailed shortly after midnight of the fourteenth. Two mornings later she was unloading in fine weather at Cambridge Bay. When the freight was discharged, the fuel tanks were topped off and the empty drums stowed below and filled with water.

"That's a lot of ballast, Skipper. Expecting heavy weather?"

"Yah." From years of preparing himself to make a Northwest Passage voyage, Larsen had learned that most of the

125

earlier expeditions had failed between Cambridge Bay and Lancaster Sound because of storms and adverse winds. "It's only five hundred miles to Bellot Strait. If we get a break in the weather, we can be there in a week and in Halifax a month after that."

"What if we don't get a break in the weather?"

"That's why we'll be carrying dogs and winter gear."

The crew, seasoned northerners now, didn't question the wisdom of hoping for the best but preparing for the worst. Superstition kept them from taunting fate by suggesting or even thinking about spending another winter in the Arctic.

Dirty weather kept the *St. Roch* at Cambridge Bay until the morning of August 20. Proceeding eastward, she kept well off the coast of Victoria Island to avoid shoals. The nights were darkening again. Not caring to navigate blindly through strange waters, Larsen ordered the vessel anchored at nine P.M. south of Jenny Lind Island. A northwest gale brought snow in the night, and the *St. Roch* pitched and rolled to the anchors until the weather moderated on the twenty-fourth.

"Left anchorage 4:15 a.m. Proceeded in southeasterly direction. Picked up and followed southward of Geographical Society Islands. Noon, abreast of Nordenskiold Island. Proceeding carefully, taking continuous soundings around large shoal patches which can be seen from the masthead. 5:00 p.m., anchored off Etah Islands, a small group about fourteen miles N.E. from Nordenskiold Island. Weather fine and clear.

"Monday, August 25.—Thick wet fog during early morning. 9:00 a.m., proceeded under way, N.N.E. direction, soundings regularly taken. No bottom at ten fathoms. 11:30, sighted King William Island, proceeded towards and followed coast eastward very cautiously as poor visibility. 2:00 p.m., approaching Simpson Strait, encountering good water, but several shoals seen. 3:33, anchored inside of islands, put motor launch over and commenced taking soundings."

All navigation was by dead reckoning based on skills Henry Larsen had learned during his Arctic years. Once a course was decided upon, they could follow it accurately by sighting back along the wake of the ship. The movements of swells over the sea were usually in a constant direction, so these were often used as a guide by which to steer. Curious birds, flying out to meet the ship, came from the nearest land, revealing positions of islands hours before they rose above the horizon. The most dependable aid, the lead line, was constantly plunking overside. When no bottom was found at ten fathoms the *St. Roch* steamed at normal cruising speed. In less water she slowed.

The lookout sighted King William Island before noon August 25. *St. Roch* followed the coast eastward slowly because of poor visibility. As she approached Simpson Strait, several shoals showed. Extreme caution was in order. No ship of the *St. Roch*'s draft was known ever to have navigated this passage. In midafternoon the anchor went down in the Etah Islands. Larsen ordered the motor launch put over and soundings taken from it to chart a channel before proceeding.

A westerly wind with fog and mist kept the ship at anchor the next day. The morning of August 27 she went on and at noon the *St. Roch* entered Peterson Bay and dropped anchor where the *Gjoa* had anchored thirty-eight years before.

Henry Larsen stood in the rain looking around at Gjoa Haven, where Roald Amundsen and his crew had been frozen in for two years. "I finally got here," he said.

Foster was nearby. "Something you've always wanted to do, Skipper?"

"Yah."

Bad weather kept the *St. Roch* at Gjoa Haven for three days. The engine was checked. More oil was transferred to the tanks and the empty drums put in the hold and filled with ballast. The crew visited the Hudson's Bay trading post ashore, and Larsen conferred with the manager, Mr. Learmonth, and local natives about conditions to the north. They could report little except that the ice had gone out later than usual.

Larsen had not yet decided what route to take to get around Boothia Peninsula and Somerset Island—the barrier between the Eastern and the Western Arctic. There were three choices: M'Clintock Channel, Peel Sound, and Bellot Strait. On the charts M'Clintock appeared the most logical way to go. Shown as a wide seaway between Victoria and Prince of Wales Islands, it led to Melville Sound and Barrow Strait, then to Lancaster Sound and Baffin Bay.

What charts did not show were the turbulent currents pouring down from the north and up from the south carrying ice packs. Meeting in treacherous cross tides, the colliding floes ground one another to bits and destroyed anything caught between. Sergeant Larsen knew of these conditions and would go by way of M'Clintock Channel only if there was no other way out. He had no desire to risk the fate of the *Erebus* and *Terror*.

Two courses remained: one by way of Peel Sound to Barrow Strait, the other through Bellot Strait, a narrow channel 250 miles to the north, separating Boothia Peninsula from Somerset Island. Bellot led from Franklin Strait seventeen miles to Prince Regent Inlet. The Hudson's Bay post at the strait's eastern end, Fort Ross, reported by wireless that Bellot and Prince Regent were still clear of ice.

Larsen weighed the advantages against the hazards of the routes. "Amundsen got through Peel Sound without much trouble."

"And the *Fort St. James* brought supplies here that way in '28," Mr. Learmonth said, "and went back the same way two years later. I guess there's nothing to it in a good ice year."

"Yah, but this isn't a good ice year." Larsen studied the

chart. "Bellot Strait would cut off three hundred miles."

"I know that M'Clintock tried five times to get the *Fox* through in 1858 and 1859, and didn't make it."

"But the *Fox* had no power and she was a deep ship."

"The *Aklavik* went to Fort Ross and back through Bellot in '37."

"She only draws eight feet, and our draft is twelve and a half."

"Whichever way you go, you'll be at the mercy of the ice, Sergeant. You've got a Hobson's choice—you'll take what's available to you."

The *St. Roch* left Gjoa Haven on the morning of August 30 and followed the King William coast through Rae Strait until early afternoon. As she neared Point Matheson, a wind came out of the northwest bringing heavy rain and mist. She anchored in a lee to await improvement.

Everyone knew the reputation of the waters ahead. They were just a day's cruising from where the *Terror* and *Erebus* had been abandoned nearly a hundred years before. King William Bay was on the other side of the island. The bones of some of Franklin's men had been found there. But the season was early, and up to now little ice had been seen. Two days of good sailing could get them to Fort Ross if they went by Bellot Strait. Via the Peel Sound route it would take a few days longer to get past this most dangerous stretch of the Northwest Passage.

The ship tossed for two days and a night in the exposed anchorage. On Monday, September 1, Larsen recorded in the log: "4:40 a.m., proceeded under way. 8:00, approaching Cape Porter. 10:05, saw large shallow patch off Dundas Island, shortly after ran into shallow water between Matty Island and Spence Bay. Vessel turned about and proceeded back and forth slowly in search of deeper water. 2:45 p.m., encountered solid icepack extending from Matty Island to Cape Christian. 3:45, anchored close to ice, current very

129

strong and ice moving with terrific rate, grinding and crushing. 6:30, changed anchorage close to small inlet. Strong westerly wind and snowfall."

And on September 2: "At anchor. Strong snowstorm from the east, impossible to see. Dropped both anchors to hold vessel as heavy floes crash against bow. 5:30 a.m., hove in starboard anchor to keep from fouling as ice commences milling around; dense fog and snowdrift. 12:25, pack setting down on vessel; changed anchorage close as possible to beach in lee of grounded ice; examined small cove for shelter, but found to be too risky to enter. Wind increasing in violence. No visibility."

A crewman, feeling conditions could hardly worsen, said, "Do you think we'll get any farther, Skipper?"

"We're only a hundred miles from Bellot Strait and it's early. A good southerly could send most of this ice back north again."

"I hope so. I don't think I could stand another winter frozen in."

"Let's hope we won't have to."

In the morning the weather moderated and visibility improved enough for the *St. Roch* to continue northward inside grounded ice near the Boothia shore. She encountered several shoals, but the depth was generally good and she made fair progress. Snow on the land made the shore hard to distinguish from the ice. The wind shifted to the west again and began pushing the pack toward the beach. At seven P.M., in a heavy snowstorm, the ship crept in behind a point for shelter from the ice and anchored close to the shore of Pasley Bay.

In the morning Larsen went ashore and climbed a hill to observe conditions to seaward. As far as he could see ice was against the coast and the entrance to the bay was blocked.

"What do you think now, Skipper? Will a southerly clear that?"

"We'll be lucky to find a winter anchorage."

"Do you suppose there's any danger of losing the ship?"

"In ice you're always in danger of losing your ship."

"What happens if we have to abandon?"

"We'll try to get to shore and head for Fort Ross on foot. Let's get back. That stuff is pushing into the bay, and I wouldn't want to be marooned here."

In the afternoon, ice was being forced into the anchorage and the *St. Roch* was moved farther up the bay. She was soon surrounded and being shoved toward shore. Larsen ordered both anchors dropped and the engine run at full throttle, but the ice still pushed her backward.

All night long the pack shoved the ship along with anchors dragging and engine running. At daybreak they tried to blast free, but the ice was held too firmly together by new snow. The pack finally grounded on a point of land and the drifting ceased. In the afternoon the pressure slackened enough to untangle the snarled anchor chains and move the ship farther from the beach. The wind was gusty, and it was still snowing hard. The men unharnessed the dogs and loaded emergency supplies and equipment on sleds in case the ship should have to be abandoned.

"Who ever heard of going over the side in a dogsled instead of a lifeboat?" someone yelled into the wind.

"You wouldn't get far in a lifeboat!"

The ice was milling and tumbling in the current. "What makes you think we'll get far with a sled?"

The pack began to drift again in the night, carrying the vessel with anchors down and engine roaring. At four in the morning the water shallowed to seven feet. The ship, with both anchors and ninety fathoms of chain dragging, was shoved over the shoal, turned twice around and listed violently from side to side.

In the engine room, Foster stood braced between a stanchion and a bulkhead, listening grimly to the creak of strain-

131

ing timbers and the grind of the keel across the bottom. To Peters he yelled, "Better get topside, George!"

"Isn't she going to hold together?"

"If she doesn't and you're still down here, your girl will be a widow before she's even married! Get out of here!"

"How about you?"

"It's my watch. Beat it!"

But beyond the shoal the water deepened. The ship came back to an even keel. The anchors were heaved. By seven A.M. the crew had worked her to the west side of the bay and reanchored. There she was icebound for two days. The open water was filled with slush, and the continuing westerly wind forced the pack against the coast, filling every bay and inlet. New ice began to form between the old floes. It snowed incessantly. The crew was kept busy shoveling off the decks.

In the morning of the second day the wind was from the southeast. The temperature began to rise. Rain began to fall. For a time hopes of getting out rose. Ice was still bearing down from seaward, and the ship was moved to deeper water near the beach. In the evening the temperature dropped again and new ice began to form.

By morning the bay was tightly packed and it was snowing. Hopes went down. The men led moorings to the beach fore and aft and dropped both anchors.

On the twelfth of September the weather cleared, and ice was forming rapidly. Larsen mustered the crew. "No use kidding ourselves, boys. We're stuck."

Ottawa was so notified by wireless. Orders were received for the detachment to take a census of the region during the coming winter. Studying maps and charts, Larsen said: "That's a big job. It will keep us busy."

A day later the vessel was frozen in solid. The Mounties explored the land in the vicinity for lakes and spent the next few days preparing for the winter. They took the water-filled drums from the hold, and emptied and stacked them on the beach. Cutting the ice away from the hull, they maneuvered the vessel to a more suitable position close to a large floe fifty yards from shore in six and a half fathoms of water. The running gear and sails were taken down and stowed. The scow and boats were landed on the ice. The dog line was stretched and the animals tied beside the ship. Excess coal was unloaded and the ice cut from around the lightened vessel so she would buoy up.

On Friday, September 19, Henry Larsen closed the ship's log for 1941. "Vessel now set for the winter. During the season we were much obstructed by ice and generally bad winds and weather, also a very early freezeup, and we were fortunate in being able to get in the present position. Total distance for season, 1,666 miles. Steaming time, 280 hours, 11 minutes."

It was just fifty days since the *St. Roch* had broken out of Walker Bay.

THE *St. Roch* had not been long in winter quarters when Eskimo hunters discovered her and set the "mukluk telegraph" in operation. Soon the snowhouses of nomadic families, with howling dogs and laughing children, were set up on the ice around the ship.

The Boothia Peninsula natives were the most primitive the *St. Roch* men had ever seen. But there was no problem of communication. They spoke virtually the same language, except for local dialects, as did all the Eskimos along the Arctic coast. Once they lost their shyness they were talkative and readily answered questions about the country and themselves.

Of these people Larsen later wrote: "The Eskimos who have the hardest life are probably the few scattered groups living around Boothia and Adelaide Peninsulas, and in the King William Island regions; they are also the most primitive. Owing to the lack of caribou, on which they depend for clothing, they nearly always seem to be ragged and dirty. In the spring and summer they mostly go inland in search of deer, returning again to the sea-ice in the fall in order to hunt seals, which are their main source of food and fuel during the long winter. Some years when they have failed in the deer hunt, one can find them huddled together in miserable little snow huts, just eking out an existence, waiting for

134

spring. The best of the clothing, in many cases the sleeping skins, have to be made over for the men, in order that they may stay out on the ice to spear seals at the breathing holes, or jig for tom cods, a small specie of codfish, hardly more than a head with a tail attached to it.

"The women and children have to stay around the snow-houses, sometimes clothed only in dirty old deerskin rags, many times with parts of their bodies exposed. Under such conditions they cannot travel very far in search of better hunting. Whatever game is secured is divided by the wife of the lucky hunter and given to the other women in camp. They all share alike; no one seems to keep anything extra for themselves; everybody is free to visit each other's snow-house and help themselves to any food or meat laying around. Sometimes they all congregate in one snowhouse and eat the food. The precious seal blubber used to cook the meat is conserved that way. . . .

"One cannot help but like and admire the Eskimos; especially so the more primitive groups among them whom we have contacted; their helpfulness to one another, their resourcefulness in hard times, and their fondness for children. As far as I have seen there is no such thing as the unwanted step-child. If a child's parents die or are unable to care for it, the child is immediately adopted by some one who can, and he fares the same as their own children. In their primitive way of life they need one another in order to hunt, live and exist. Some of their customs perhaps do not agree with our way of thinking, but they are no worse than many among civilized people."

When there were hard times in the Arctic, the R.C.M.P. often heard rumors of old and feeble Eskimos or babies being put to death so as not to be a burden on their people. Such cases were hard to prove, but suicides among the elderly in times of need were common. The Mounties received a report about a man who had lost the use of his legs and could no longer hunt. He ordered members of his family to

135

shoot him. When they refused, he strangled himself with the line on his seal spear. The body was wrapped in a skin and dragged to a rocky islet and left there. The camp was then moved to a new location to be away from the tragedy site and the spirit believed to lurk there.

Visiting the camp a few days later, Larsen was told of the incident and went to the islet to examine the body and confirm the story. On his way back, a snowstorm came up. When he reached the camp the natives said that the blow was sent by the dead man's spirit because Larsen had disturbed him.

An Eskimo named Equalla came to Pasley Bay from Gjoa Haven to bring an outboard motor for repair by Jack Foster. Intelligent and cheerful, he was hired as a guide and went on all major patrols during the winter of 1941–1942. The first of these went out to Bellot Strait and Fort Ross to locate native camps in preparation for the spring census. Larsen and Equalla left the ship on December 2, were gone twenty-one days, and covered 320 miles.

On January 5, 1942, Chartrand and Equalla left for Gjoa Haven to establish a fish cache and have new winter clothing made for the detachment by King William Land natives. They reached Gjoa Haven in eight days and put up at the Hudson's Bay Company house.

Chartrand built the fish cache and arranged with local families to make the clothing. Equalla continued on to Simpson Strait to visit his people and have clothes made for himself. During his absence, Frenchy Chartrand spent his time repairing equipment and dog harness and visiting the natives. They were in good health, game was plentiful, and trapping was good. Equalla returned on the twentieth, but bad weather kept them at Gjoa Haven for six more days. They got back to the *St. Roch* on the first of February. In twenty-eight days, they had trailed 489 miles.

The detachment had received a message in January from Cambridge Bay that John Friederich was leaving on patrol to King William Land and planned to go on to Pasley Bay to visit them. Weeks passed and he did not arrive, nor did Gjoa Haven report his appearance. Word finally came through that he was back at Cambridge Bay. He had been unable to complete the patrol because his guide refused to go beyond Queen Maud Gulf and the interpreter got sick.

In February the wireless reported that Friederich himself was sick. He had been having pains in his abdomen, and the condition was reported by radio to a doctor in Aklavik. When the pains worsened and settled in his right side, the doctor said, "You've got appendicitis, John. We'll have to get you out of there."

The nearest hospital was at Fort Smith, 650 miles away on the northern border of Alberta. Aklavik was even farther. Transporting a man with an inflamed appendix by dogsled such a distance was impossible, and because of the war no aircraft or pilots were left in the North. What happens to him now? Hadley wondered after monitoring messages between Ottawa, Aklavik, and Cambridge Bay.

"They'll get him out of there," Larsen said. "The R.C.M.P. always takes care of its people."

An airplane was finally located at Sioux Lookout, Ontario, fifteen hundred miles south of Cambridge Bay. The pilot, who had never flown in the Far North before, loaded his ship with tins of gasoline and found the destination by homing in on its wireless signal. He picked up Friederich and took him to Fort Smith. There the appendix was removed, and he recovered quickly.

Frenchy Chartrand wasn't so lucky. After returning from King William Land he began having stomach pains. Assuming that something he had eaten had disagreed with him, he took baking soda and felt a little better. In the forecastle on the evening of February 13 he gasped, clutched at his chest, toppled over with a heart attack, and died. He was thirty-seven years old.

The detachment, always prepared for the loss of a man to

the dangers of the Arctic, found sudden death by a natural cause hard to accept. Each time a person left the *St. Roch* it was expected that he might never be seen alive again. Drowning in the surf, freezing on a winter trail, being turned on by dogs, a fatal gunshot, or mauling by a polar bear were all hazards. But the unexpected flickering out of the seemingly hardiest life among them was unnerving.

"That's fate for you," Farrar said when Larsen declared Chartrand dead. "Frenchy was just telling me that when his enlistment was up he was going to marry a girl back home."

They built a coffin, bathed Frenchy's body, dressed it in his working clothes, and put his rosary in his hands. "There's a Catholic priest living with the Eskimos at Pelly Bay," Larsen said. "When we make the census patrol I'll go there and see if he'll come and bury Frenchy."

The lid was nailed down and the coffin stowed in the hold until milder weather permitted the digging of a grave on shore.

The detachment was already making preparations for the patrol around the Boothia Peninsula to take the census. The day before departure two sleds were loaded with precooked food for the men and dried fish and canned tallow for the dogs. Primus stoves and kerosine, snow knives, cooking pots, and rifles were put on top of the loads and the canvas covers lashed down.

The patrol left on the morning of February 24. Equalla led the way with his seven dogs pulling the smaller sled, breaking trail in soft, deep snow. Larsen and Hunt followed, driving eleven police dogs hitched to the big komatik. They were prepared to be gone two months and travel a thousand miles. Besides taking the census, they were to investigate conditions among the Eskimos.

It took eight days to reach Fort Ross. The weather generally was calm and clear, but soft snow made travel slow, averaging less than twenty-five miles a day. The men took turns walking ahead on snowshoes, breaking trail for the teams and sleds. Leaving Hunt to take the census at the camps on Brentford Bay, Larsen and Equalla pushed on up Somerset Island. Fair weather made traveling good, and they covered thirty-five miles before making camp at Cape Garry. Here they saw an ancient settlement of houses framed with whalebone and covered with stones and earth. Ribs were sticking from the ground, and there were whale skulls around.

Continuing on the next day, they followed old trails to a camp on the north shore of Creswell Bay—four small, filthy houses inhabited by dirty, smelly natives. After taking the census, Larsen asked about the ruins seen the day before. He was told that they were the remains of Tunit villages.

"What are Tunits?"

"They were the people who lived here before the Eskimos. They were very big and went to sea in large boats and killed whales. They used different tools and weapons than we do. We still find their things, and it's easy to tell whether an Eskimo or a Tunit made it."

"What did these Tunits look like?"

"They are dead too long ago. Nobody can remember."

"What happened to them?"

"When the Eskimos came there were big fights and we killed them."

"Does anyone know what their boats were like?"

"All gone too long ago. We still go to the Tunit houses and get whalebone to put on the runners of our sleds."

No camps were known to exist north of Creswell Bay, so the patrol turned back south in the morning. At Cape Esther another group of mounds was found with whalebones sticking from them and skulls around. Larsen examined the ruins for a time before going on.

Reaching Fort Ross the next evening, the Mounties stayed there over Sunday, resting the dogs and drying

139

clothes. They left at noon on Monday, traveling to Brentford Bay where Hunt was. There they spent the next day butchering seals for dog feed. While they worked, Larsen told Hunt about the ancient villages to the north. "The people who lived there were farther advanced than the Eskimos, since they lived in houses and hunted whales. I hope someday the Government sends people to excavate some of those old settlements."

"What do you think they'd find there?"

"Evidence that the Tunits were the descendants of the Vikings who disappeared from Greenland and Vinland a thousand years ago."

They left Brentford Bay on the morning of March 11 and went to a native camp on the ice. As at every settlement, they were welcomed heartily, invited in, and offered the best of whatever might be simmering in the cooking pot. The elder lady of the household would feel around in the pot with a grimy hand, bring out a delicacy, lick it off, and give it to the visitors. The practice of the Mounties was to slice off a small piece and toss the rest back. Though Larsen wasn't squeamish about food, he liked to know what he was eating. This time the sad-eyed head of a moustached seal stared back when he looked in the pot.

After taking the census of the camp the three men went on. The weather was mild, but it began to snow and they came upon rough ice. The next day a south wind began to drift the snow and make visibility too poor for travel. When they did push on, deep drifts made pulling hard and the damp snow balled up on the dogs' feet. Sunday evening they got to Arviktootsiak, 125 miles south of Fort Ross.

Entering the snow village near Lord Mayor Bay, the patrol heard a commotion in the largest of the houses. After caring for the dogs, the Mounties crawled through the entrance passage and saw a huge white man, wearing bearskin pants and parka, playing a concertina and singing

140

"Shall We Gather at the River." All around him Eskimos stood and squatted, singing the hymn in their native tongue. When Hunt and Larsen were recognized as whites, the music stopped. The bearded musician introduced himself as Canon Turner, an Anglican missionary from Pond Inlet, Baffin Island, five hundred miles away. He had arrived the day before on his yearly visit.

The newcomers shook hands with everyone, including babies in their mothers' parkas, and the services continued. It was mostly singing, and the policemen joined in. Several hours of exuberant rejoicing created so much heat that the roof caved in. Since the weather was mild, it was not considered worthwhile to rebuild the house in the dark, so the feasting began.

Everybody contributed something. The Eskimos brought frozen fish and seal meat. Mr. Turner cooked a pot of rolled oats. The Mounties donated tea and sugar and the use of their primus stoves.

When the eating was finished and news exchanged, it was after three in the morning. Canon Turner, Sergeant Larsen, and Constable Hunt lay down on the sleeping platform with an Eskimo family on each side.

Between the crying of babies and the snoring of adults, sleep was fitful. Larsen and Hunt were just dozing off at daybreak when they were awakened by the concertina. The missionary was holding morning services in the middle of the roofless snowhouse. The tired policemen, lulled by the chanting of the natives, drifted off again and slept until they were awakened by the canon serving bowls of oatmeal. He was about to leave for home by way of Fort Ross.

Of their meeting with Mr. Turner, Larsen wrote: "At this spot the North-West Passage was again completed. Canon Turner came from England and had arrived from an east coast port of Canada, coming to Baffin Island on the . . . steamer 'Nascopie,' and crossed over to Boothia by dogs.

We had arrived from Vancouver to the west side of Boothia, then traveled around it by dogs. Our meeting with Canon Turner was purely one of chance, neither of us knew of the other's movements."

The bearskin-clad missionary raced away from Arviktootsiak behind his team and sled and vanished in a snowstorm. Larsen and Hunt spent the rest of the day taking the census and inquiring about the drowning of a seal hunter. It was calm and still snowing heavily when they broke camp in the morning. Again, damp snow balled up on the dogs' feet and made them bleed when they traveled over rough ice. It took three days to reach Thom Bay, eighty miles away.

The Eskimo settlement was the largest the Mounties had seen on the east coast of Boothia. The people were primitive, living much as their ancestors must have lived when John Ross came in 1829, searching for the Northwest Passage. His vessel, the *Victory*, had been the first steamship in the Canadian Arctic. Crude and inefficient, the bulky, coal-burning engine had turned out to be a liability and was dismantled and sent ashore to make more room aboard the vessel. After being frozen in for three years and with food almost gone, Ross abandoned the ship in the spring of 1832. He and his crew were rescued by another vessel of the expedition.

The Thom Bay natives were the healthiest seen on the trip. Seal and fish were plentiful, but everyone was poorly clothed because of a deerskin shortage.

On a ten-mile trip to Victoria Harbour the patrol visited the site of the *Victory*'s abandonment. They found large iron plates and bolts that had been parts of the ship's boiler and steam engine, coils of hemp rope almost as good as new after more than a hundred years on the arctic beach, and an old bronze cannon that Larsen wanted to take to the *St. Roch*. But it was too heavy to load on the sled. "It breaks my heart to leave it here."

They made a search for a cairn recorded in Ross's journal as having been built there, but found no sign of it. Nor did anything remain of the *Victory* herself.

Back at Thom Bay older people, telling stories handed down by their fathers, described the explorers and ship in detail. The vessel, they said, had finally drifted out of the harbor and was crushed by ice and sunk near an island in Lord Mayor Bay. Every family in the region still used tools and blubber lamps made from parts of the boiler and engine.

Equalla didn't know the way to Pelly Bay, so he was sent on alone to King William Land. The Mounties would meet him later at Gjoa Haven. A local native was hired to guide the patrol. They left Thom Bay the morning of March 23 and late in the day met another native and camped with him on the ice. He took them sealing in the evening. The next day they traveled to his camp off Cape Kjer. In spite of a northeast wind, drifting snow, and no visibility, he found the camp with little effort. There were three snowhouses there and Larsen and Hunt were invited to stay at one of them. During the night a blizzard blew holes in the house, filling everything with snow. The holes had to be patched and snow beaten out of clothes and sleeping robes before anyone could sleep again.

In the morning the census was taken. Seals were abundant in a nearby open lead, and the natives were well fed.

High winds and driving snow kept the Mounties at the camp for three days. On the twenty-eighth the wind moderated and they traveled forty miles. Another storm blew up in the night and they huddled cold and comfortless in camp all day. On the thirtieth they made thirty-five miles, and on the next day, fifty-five, reaching Father Gustav Henri's mission on Kellett River at ten in the evening.

The priest, big and powerful-looking with a flaming red beard, attributed his good health and strength to eating what the Eskimos ate—seal meat and raw frozen fish. The mission was in a small stone house, about sixteen feet by twenty-four, built by the father himself of hundreds of rocks held together with clay. The room where he ate and slept was partitioned off with wood and skins and heated by a stove in which he burned seal blubber and moss. A pleasant, generous man, he turned over his quarters to the Mounties, insisting that he sleep on the floor himself.

The priest offered wine to the tired visitors, but the keg was frozen and had to be thawed. The warming wine and weariness made Larsen and Hunt fall asleep while Father Henri was saying midnight Mass. When they awakened, he had already held his morning service and was getting breakfast. They excused themselves for sleeping through the services. The priest laughed. "It's only right that you should sleep like good Protestants while I pray for you."

Larsen told him of Frenchy's death. "Would it be possible for you to come to Pasley Bay and hold a funeral service?"

"I'll be glad to, but it will have to be later in the spring when the seals come out on the ice to sleep in the sun. It will be easier to get dog feed then."

At Father Henri's suggestion, the patrol decided not to continue on to take the census of the region. Everyone would be coming to the mission to attend Easter rites the following Sunday and could be counted then. Teams began arriving. By Saturday a village of new snowhouses had sprung up around the mission.

In his journal Larsen recorded: "On Easter morning we joined in the service, attended by about 80 Eskimos of all ages, packed into the little stone building. There was no room and nothing for them to sit on, so they were nearly all standing up, except for a few old ones who squatted on the floor. The Father had taught hymns and prayers to these people, and the service was held in the Eskimo language. The Father looked wonderful in his robes. He is a fine big man . . . and the Eskimos just love him.

"While the service was going on, a great pile of fish was thawing in one corner, and a large pot of meat was simmering over a seal oil lamp, so as to be ready for feasting immediately the service was over. A young woman next to me fainted twice, but nobody paid any attention to her as they were too busy singing. Each time I dragged her outside into the fresh air, and when she came to she just smiled and shuffled in again. I found out afterwards that she had just come about 100 miles and had given birth to a baby a few hours before the service.

"After the service they immediately began to rejoice, which took the form of eating. The Father introduced us to them as King George's men who had come especially to visit them, and told them to give us a hearty Eskimo welcome. This they did with great shouts between each mouthful. We were the first policemen to visit these people, so to give a good impression we contributed a case of beef tallow that we carried along as emergency dogfeed. The Eskimos are exceedingly fond of this kind of tallow. It is just pure edible beef tallow which we use ourselves on the trail instead of lard. At once the Eskimos began to cut the tallow up in pieces and they crunched large chunks of it as dessert.

"After the feast they had games outside for the men; this consisted mainly of throwing a harpoon at a snowblock, and shooting with bow and arrow. They all have rifles now, but the Father encourages them to keep up practice with bow and arrow, which I think is a good thing. I was selected to be the judge, and as such it was my duty to hand out the prizes to the winners. The Father had some small prizes, and Corporal [sic] Hunt and I donated some of our tobacco and cigarette papers, and a pair of snow glasses, which I intended as first prize. Every man was to shoot three arrows each. Some of the older men were quite good, but there was a handsome young fellow that I thought should have first prize. He therefore got the snow glasses.

145

"We soon found out that we didn't have enough prizes to go around as each man came up for a prize whether he had made a good score or not. No Eskimo considers himself inferior to another; for had he not tried just as hard to hit the target? He had just had bad luck with his shooting, that was all. Sometimes it was the same way with the hunting. Some days certain Eskimos got game, then some other days other Eskimos got the game. They all received the benefits from it, so why should they not all get a prize, which is perhaps a good way of reasoning. We therefore had to resort to a few more pounds of tallow, which we cut in halves, thus each man received a prize. Strangely enough, the ones who got the real prizes would rather have had the tallow."

That evening when they turned in, Hunt complained of a sore throat. "Too much singing, I guess."

They said good-by to Father Henri and his congregation in the morning. The first leg of the journey to King William Land was by way of the seal camp on the ice to pick up dog feed and a guide. It was forty-five miles to the camp. They got there at ten o'clock that night. Hunt's throat was worse, and he was coming down with a cold. Larsen's throat was getting sore too. "We must have picked it up at that celebration yesterday."

They left the seal camp at noon the next day guided by a young man named Kalvik. Following the west coast of Pelly Bay southward, they camped at seven thirty in the evening at the Becher River. By now Larsen had caught the cold, and both men were feeling miserable. In the morning they went on, following the twisting river, passing lakes and frozen rapids. Hard snow crystals cut the dogs' feet badly.

Traveling against a strong west wind and heavy ground drift, they managed to reach Simpson Lake, thirty miles from the coast, before they called it quits. Both were sick and weak and weary.

Unable to travel because of a blizzard, Hunt and Larsen

spent the next day shivering under sleeping robes in a snow-house built by Kalvik. In midmorning of April 10, though still sick and exhausted, they pushed on into the cold west wind. The weather and their weakened condition made progress slow. It took four more days of wretched sledding to reach salt water at the mouth of the Murchison River. The sea ice was smooth, and traveling was good. They forced themselves on until eight o'clock before stopping for the night.

In the morning the weather was clear and bright with a bitter west wind blowing across the ice. Though still weak and shaky, Hunt and Larsen staggered on, reaching Gjoa Haven on the evening of April 15. At the Hudson's Bay post they were immediately put to bed by Mr. Learmonth. Besides his nagging cold, Hunt was suffering the stabbing pains of snow blindness from squinting into the dazzling sunlight reflecting off the ice.

The two Mounties spent two weeks at Gjoa Haven, recovering from illness and regaining strength. At last they departed with a guide, Ooshoogalak, and encountered rough ice and thawing snow all the way to Pasley Bay. It took a week to go the 150 miles. They were back aboard the *St. Roch* on May 6 after having been gone seventy-one days and traveling 1,140 miles.

It was the last patrol of the year.

[14]

RISING SPRINGTIME TEMPERATURES made it necessary to inter the body of Frenchy before Father Henri came from Pelly Bay. A grave was dug on a hill overlooking the anchorage, and the coffin was sledded ashore and buried. When the priest arrived and the funeral service was over, a cairn of rocks was built on the grave and a wooden cross erected. It bore a hand-lettered metal plate with the R.C.M.P. crest and an inscription: "8th October 1904—13th February 1942, Regimental No. 10155, Constable Albert Joseph Chartrand, Royal Canadian Mounted Police, Schooner St. Roch, Pasley Bay, NWT."

Father Henri stayed only a few days, then had to hurry back to his mission, 250 miles away, before the thaw impeded travel.

Mr. Learmonth made a visit too. Besides being the Hudson's Bay Company manager at Gjoa Haven, he was also a representative of the Ontario Museum. He told of another grave some miles away. Only recently found by natives, it was believed possibly to contain the bones of Sir John Franklin. Learmonth had been commissioned to examine it and try to determine if, in fact, it was the grave of Franklin.

Later Sergeant Larsen said to Foster, "They should have us do that. If that's Franklin's grave, why, Learmonth will be famous!"

"Henry, you're just an old glory hunter," Foster kidded.

He had touched a sore spot. Larsen wouldn't speak to him for weeks.

With the return of the midnight sun in early May, the breakup really set in. When summer began six weeks later, most of the snow was gone from the land, but the *St. Roch* was still icebound. Pasley Bay was solid, and to the north and south pressure ridges fifty to a hundred feet high were piled against the coast. Larsen was pessimistic and said there might be no navigation season at all that year. But the crew went ahead with preparations. They reloaded the supplies, overhauled the engine, rerigged sails, and cleaned and painted the ship.

On August 3, 1942, eleven months after the *St. Roch* had been forced into Pasley Bay, meltwater draining from the hills loosened the ice. It began going out with the tide, carrying the vessel. The engine was started, anchors hove in, and she left winter quarters in a foggy rain.

Larsen reopened the log: "3:30 p.m., left winter anchorage and proceeded to mouth of the bay with the outgoing tide. Anchored at 5:10 p.m. at the north point. Entrance blocked by ice. During the night, drift ice filled the bay.

"Tuesday, August 4.—At anchor awaiting opportunity to get out. Made several trips to nearby hill to observe ice condition. Ice appears unbroken offshore as far as can be seen. P.M., easterly wind opened small lead close to shore. 10:10 p.m., proceeded outside and made good progress until midnight when wind changed to N.W. with thick weather. Lead closing."

At one A.M. a lead opened to the westward. The *St. Roch* entered it, and tied up to a southward-drifting floe as the lead closed around her. The pressure of the pack began listing the vessel violently from side to side. Larsen ordered preparations to abandon ship. The Mounties harnessed the dogs and loaded sleds with emergency supplies. But at four o'clock the weather cleared and the drifting stopped.

149

Solidly beset again only a few miles from the point of departure, the crew were fed up with the Arctic, the ship, and one another. They defied superstition. Larsen heard open talk of not getting out this season and of the possibility of losing the *St. Roch*.

R.C.M.P. tradition forbade criticism of the commander, but there were some dark thoughts along that line too. The men had no doubts about Larsen's competence as a navigator. He had handled the ship to perfection under grave adversities and maintained her in top shape. But two years' isolation and danger twisted men's minds. They didn't reason clearly. They needed a scapegoat on whom to vent anxieties. "It was his damn dreams of glory that got us into this."

The skipper harbored some dark thoughts of his own. He knew well enough that but for him this voyage would never have been ordered. His years of promoting the Northwest Passage had led Ottawa to believe that he could take the *St. Roch* through. They had believed in him, and it seemed he was about to let them down. Sure, he had had a run of bad luck, but that wouldn't excuse him in the eyes of the historians. The name Henry Asbjorn Larsen would be just another on the list of skippers who had failed in the Arctic.

It would be easy enough to abandon ship now while the ice was all around, and to get safely to land and eventually home. But Henry Asbjorn Larsen was a bullheaded Norwegian. As long as the *St. Roch* was afloat, he was going to fight to get her through. The same streak of pride that sent him north in search of fame wouldn't let him give up and go down in history as just another failure. For the moment, though, fighting consisted of waiting and watching from the masthead to see what nature would serve up next.

Nothing happened for two days.

Just after midnight on August 6, the pack began to move. Pressure suddenly increased. Ominous creakings resounded through the ice-squeezed hull. Suddenly *St. Roch* was heeled far over to port by a floe sliding under her keel. As though in drydock, she was lifted by the floe until the stern was four feet out of the water with propeller and rudder exposed. Here she sat for a time with bow down and fantail high.

The floe finally slid from under, and the ship settled back with a splash and a roll that jammed the rudder hard over. The crew had to explode bombs and use chisels to free the rudder and keep the propeller clear. The pressure was partly relieved when the ice cracked in several places.

For the next six days the pack was all around, but there was little pressure. On the morning of August 12 the ice began to slacken. But while the ship worked toward a floe, the cooling jacket on the number one cylinder of the engine cracked and flooded.

"My God, what next!" someone growled.

The engineers blocked off the disabled cylinder, and the engine ran well enough, but with reduced power. As they were cleaning up, Peters said, "What do you suppose made that thing break, Jack?"

"The vibration of running full ahead and full astern and ramming is bound to tear something apart. I'm surprised the old bucket of bolts has held up as well as she has."

The vessel was beset again for two long days. Then the pressure began to slacken, and she started working northward. Larsen wasn't happy with the progress. "Can you give us any more revolutions, Yack?"

"She's losing too much power from that blocked-out cylinder. The only thing that will help is to shut her down and pull the piston and connecting rod so they won't drag."

"How long would it take?"

"About four hours, but we'll make it up with the extra power we get."

"Do it, then. We'll need all she's got to get to Bellot Strait."

It took four hours and five minutes to complete the repairs. Without the drag of the idle piston, the engine developed the maximum revolutions possible from five working cylinders. The *St. Roch* made a good passage through loose ice until the pack tightened up again.

The engine caused no more problems, but troubles with ice seemed to be just beginning. For the next eleven days the *St. Roch* worked back and forth, searching for a way through the ice field in which she drifted up and down M'Clintock Channel.

As they looked out over the jumble of blue and white, the scene and the situation and the thoughts of crewmen must have been very like those experienced by *Terror* and *Erebus* in this same vicinity nearly a hundred years before. The Canadians had one advantage that the Englishmen didn't have—power. But when beset, the diesel engine was as useless as had been the sails and masts of Franklin's windjammers.

Then, on August 25, as the ship was being carried westward by a strong gale, the ice suddenly split. The schooner broke free. The crew started the engine and worked eastward through the leads toward Boothia. Near midnight, stopped by ice and darkness, the ship was moored to a floe.

At daybreak she got under way toward the Tasmania Islands, just off the Boothia Peninsula at the entrance to Franklin Strait. Bellot was sixty miles away. Reaching the western end of the islands, she was stopped again by the pack. With the change of tide the ice started swinging toward the rocky shore. The Mounties cast off and went looking for safe anchorage.

At noon Larsen ordered the anchor dropped in the channel between the two westernmost of the Tasmania Islands. It was snowing, and a northwest wind was blowing. They had to keep changing position to avoid the drift ice coming through with the tides.

The next day Larsen went to the nearest island and climbed a hill. Franklin Strait was impassable all the way to Prince of Wales Island, twenty-five miles to the west.

About midnight a floe began forcing the ship broadside toward the island. Again, preparations were made to abandon ship. Dad Parry was concerned about walking any great distance. He had been having trouble with his feet all winter. "How far is it to Fort Ross, Skipper?"

"About seventy-five miles."

"I'll never make it, boys. I'll never make it!"

"Don't worry," Foster said, "I'll see that you don't suffer."

Parry eyed the chief engineer, who usually executed incurably sick or injured dogs. "You son of a gun, I think you mean it!"

They broke free while the floe was still away from the shore. A north wind began blowing a steady stream of ice down the channel. Beyond the islands they could see the pack breaking up in Franklin Strait. The wind slackened in the early morning of the twenty-ninth, and at six A.M. the *St. Roch* entered a lead. She worked westward to Dixon Island, then north until they were opposite Bellot Strait. Peel Sound was clear, and she headed east.

Sergeant Larsen later wrote: "We cut across and entered this Strait the same night. The western end of the Strait was clear of ice, but in the middle there was a barrier right across, held there by some heavy grounded ice. This Strait [Bellot] is only half a mile wide and there is a terrific current. As the ice came pouring in behind us, there was nothing else to do but crash into it and attempt to drift through. This we did; the strong current causing large whirlpools in which large cakes of ice spun and gyrated. Many times we thought the ship would crack like a nut under the pressure. Sometimes we became stationary off projecting points of land—high, dark, inaccessible cliffs— the Strait is about 18 miles long.

153

"We had two young Eskimos aboard, a man and his wife. One has to admire the quality of these people. At times when things looked really bad they would go up on the forecastle head and sing at the top of their voices. They told me they were singing so the ship wouldn't get crushed, so I told them to keep on singing. They were quite pleased after we got through, when I told them their singing had no doubt helped us a great deal.

"Meanwhile, the people at the eastern end of the Strait, at the Hudson's Bay Company post, Fort Ross, had anxiously watched our struggles, and they all came swarming aboard to welcome us. We considered our voyage practically over at this time as the Hudson's Bay Company ship 'Nascopie' has called here regularly every year since 1937. But it so happened that in 1942 it didn't reach Fort Ross owing to the ice pouring into Prince Regent Inlet after we left."

Thoroughly fed up with the North, the crew of the *St. Roch* were anxious to complete the voyage. They planned to leave first thing in the morning, but during the night a north wind brought a stream of ice down Prince Regent Inlet. The bronze cannon on the beach at Victoria Harbour would have to stay there. Larsen's concern was to get the vessel out of the Arctic before they were caught for another year.

Frequently changing anchorage to avoid ice in Depot Bay, the *St. Roch* remained at Fort Ross until the second of September. With improving weather, she got under way in the morning, following the coast of Somerset Island northward inside heavy floes. Anchoring that evening off Fury Beach, she was not far from the ruins of the Tunit villages at Creswell Bay.

Visibility was poor at daybreak when they began working leads. Ice fields and thick fog made progress slow. By noon the fog cleared, and several hours later the *St. Roch* passed the northeast cape of Somerset Island and entered Lancaster Sound. The wind was cold, and young ice was forming as she set a course for Baffin Island. By early evening the sea was clear of ice. A few hours later, encountering scattered floes, she moored to one and awaited daylight.

The weather was calm and clear but very cold, and new ice was forming when she cast off at four in the morning. Fearful of being caught at sea by an early winter, the crew set sails and, with the ailing engine turning as fast as they dared run it, the *St. Roch* slogged along at nearly seven knots. She entered Navy Board Inlet on the northeast coast of Baffin Island at sunset. At midnight the engine was shut down, and she drifted until the return of daylight.

Icebergs began appearing. Born of the great glaciers creeping down from the island's mountains, they were a novelty never seen in the Western Arctic, where there were no glaciers.

Later in the day the vessel passed her destination in a snowstorm. When the error was discovered she was brought about and backtracked until the watch saw the lights of the settlement at Albert Harbour, Pond Inlet. Again the engine was shut down, and she drifted until daylight.

After anchoring the ship off the R.C.M.P. buildings in the morning, the Mounties spent the next few days preparing for the last leg of the voyage. The dogs and sleds were sent ashore. Excess stores and coal were unloaded for use by the detachment. Drums of oil were taken aboard. Fuel tanks were filled and the empty drums stowed in the hold and filled with water to ballast the ship for the passage down stormy Baffin Bay and Davis Strait. The crew restowed the hold and trimmed the ship for sea, helped by Constable J. W. Doyle, whose tour of duty at Pond Inlet was completed and who would accompany them outside.

"Thursday, September 10.—7:00 a.m., proceeded under way. Reefed sails and lashed all boats and equipments, etc., in readiness for bad weather. Put extra tarpaulins on the main hatch. Outside of inlet strong N.E. wind and heavy swell. Vessel rolling violently, passing several large icebergs."

Two days after leaving Pond Inlet, a noon position showed that the *St. Roch* had come 932 miles since leaving Pasley Bay six weeks earlier. She was making good headway, and the next day she crossed the 69th Parallel—the dividing line between Baffin Bay and Davis Strait. Putting away his navigation instruments, Larsen commented cautiously, "We just might make it."

In Davis Strait she followed inside an ice pack studded with bergs. The big blue masses could be seen from a distance and avoided. The menace was growlers—small chunks of dense, glacial ice almost awash. These tended to lie unseen in a choppy sea until the suction of the passing vessel roused them and they bobbed up to stab violently at the disturbing hull, like angered monsters of the sea. While the *St. Roch* rode out a southeast gale with snow and little visibility, one growler surged to the surface close aboard. The *St. Roch* did not have enough power to dodge the ice, and it knocked a chunk out of the guard rail. "A foot closer and that one would have sent us to the bottom!"

Day after day the ship proceeded slowly southward through the stormy sea. Because of a heavy swell, the whole pack was in motion. It was impossible to avoid all the growlers.

On September 15 the wind moderated and the ice began to scatter. With clearing weather, the R.C.M.P. ship proceeded on over a sea illumined by a brilliant display of northern lights.

In spite of adverse weather and ice conditions, the *St. Roch* plodded on, averaging about a hundred miles a day. Passing Cape Dyer on the sixteenth, she crossed the Arctic Circle for the first time in two years and two months. A noon observation on September 19 showed her to be well south of Hudson Strait and off Saglek Bay on the east coast of Labrador, 1,719 miles from winter quarters.

In the Labrador Sea, the strain of constant rolling opened seams around the deckhouse. Green water washing aboard seeped into the saloon and engine room below. It was inconvenient, but not dangerous as long as the pumps kept working.

The first vessel the Mounties sighted was a fishing schooner off Roundhill Island, Newfoundland, making for port in a southeast gale. A fisherman was engaged to pilot the *St. Roch* into Bateau Harbour. She anchored on the afternoon of the twenty-second, where she lay for four days. Bucking head-on winds, the ship then worked through the Strait of Belle Isle into the Gulf of St. Lawrence.

Sergeant Larsen wasn't happy with the performance of the engine. On the last day of September, getting low on fresh water, he set a course for the Bay of Islands on the west coast of the island of Newfoundland. The following morning the *St. Roch* moored to the wharf of the Bowaters paper mill at Corner Brook. Water was taken on, and arrangements were made with the engineers of the mill to repair the cylinder head that had broken in Franklin Strait.

The repairs were completed on October 3, and two days later the ship sailed from Corner Brook with a wartime convoy. In the afternoon the convoy outdistanced the *St. Roch* in a freshening westerly wind. Steaming on alone, she pitched and rolled for two days in Cabot Strait. On October 7, St. Paul Island was sighted. A few hours later the *St. Roch* anchored in South Harbour, Nova Scotia, so the crew could get some sleep. Sailing again early in the morning, she reached Sydney at nine o'clock. After taking aboard a pilot, she entered the Bras d'Or Lakes, then went through St. Peters locks and reached the Atlantic Ocean at last on the afternoon of the tenth.

The next day Sergeant Larsen made his last entry of the voyage in the *St. Roch*'s logbook:

"Sunday, October 11th. Fine weather and good speed during the night. 1:10 p.m., Halifax Harbour pilot aboard. 1:20, anchored outside gate awaiting instruction. Inspectors Mortimer, Curleigh, Archer and Chard boarded the vessel here. 3:30 p.m., tied up alongside Kings Wharf and thus completed the first navigation of the Northwest Passage from West to East from Vancouver, B. C., to Halifax, N. S. Total mileage this season, 2,839 miles. Steaming hours, 551 hours, 38 minutes."

[15]

GEORGE PETERS' NURSE was still waiting, and they were married. Commissioner Wood, who had been instrumental in having the *St. Roch* designed and built, came to Halifax to inspect her and congratulate the crew. "She has certainly justified herself," the trim old Mountie said. "Would you like to do it again, Sergeant?"

"Only if she had a bigger engine, sir. I still think we'd have made it in one season if she'd had the power to buck the pack."

"We'll see what we can do about that before you sail again."

"Do you have any plans for us yet, sir?"

"Next year you will supply our Eastern Arctic detachments."

King George VI approved the awarding of the Silver Polar Medal to Larsen, Foster, Parry, Farrar, Peters, Hunt, and Hadley, and to Chartrand posthumously. And Henry Larsen was promoted to staff sergeant.

The crew went home for long furloughs, and the vessel was taken to Lunenberg, Nova Scotia, for dry-docking. Two years of being frozen in and all her encounters with ice packs and growlers had hardly marred the ironbark sheathing. The hull needed little more than cleaning and painting. She got no change of engines.

The 1943 patrol of the Eastern Arctic was uneventful. When the *St. Roch* entered Hudson Strait most of the ice was gone, and Larsen had no trouble navigating the unfamiliar region. They returned to Halifax in October after cruising nearly 7,500 miles.

Orders were received from Ottawa for the following year: Return to Vancouver by way of the northern route of the Northwest Passage! The *St. Roch* would sail a course through Lancaster Sound, Barrow Strait, Melville Sound, and Prince of Wales Strait. Other than to call at Frobisher Bay and resupply Pond Inlet, few police duties would be involved. It was not a publicity stunt, but an assignment of great importance to the future of Canada.

War and the development of long-range aircraft and giant icebreakers had made the government acutely conscious of the value of the Far North. Geologists believed oil and mineral reserves there were without limit. Some years earlier the explorer Sverdrup had laid claim to a few of the more remote northern islands in the name of Norway. A sum of money had been paid by Canada for the relinquishment of Sverdrup's claims. Since then some Canadians in high places had become concerned lest their nation not be able to uphold its territorial rights in the Arctic against a stronger country. It would be the duty of the *St. Roch* to reestablish Canada's sovereignty over the Arctic Islands. Stops would be made at strategic points and evidence left of Canada's claim to the region.

In preparing for the voyage in early 1944, there was no governmental penny-pinching so far as requests for equipment were concerned. Some of the heavy wartime expenditures were allowed to trickle down to the *St. Roch*. She was equipped with a modern gyrocompass and finally got the heavy-duty power plant the captain and engineers had been pleading for since 1928. A three-hundred-horsepower diesel was installed. The old engine, still in good condition, was sold and shipped west to power a salmon seiner. The vessel later sank off the Aleutian Islands, taking with her to the bottom the engine that had served the *St. Roch* dependably for sixteen years.

With the doubling of her power, the R.C.M.P. ship at last became a true motor vessel with auxiliary sails. The tall mainmast that had added to her rolling propensities was replaced with a stubby pole abaft the stack to support the wireless antenna. To contain the larger engine and equipment to operate the electric gyrocompass, the engine room was extensively remodeled, as were the after living quarters and the deckhouse. For more warmth and comfort, the stern was enclosed except for a small area on the fantail left open for handling lines.

The modernized *St. Roch* carried a crew of eleven when she sailed from the Dartmouth shipyards on July 19, 1944. Besides Larsen, only three were members of the R.C.M.P. Peters and Hunt, corporals now, were chief engineer and clerk-seaman, respectively, and Constable J. M. Diplock was a seaman. The others were special constables, experienced seafarers hired to fill out the complement. The mate, Ollie Andreasen, had spent thirty years in the Arctic. He had been with Stefansson when he had crossed the Beaufort Sea ice on foot with only a few dogs to haul their camping equipment. R. T. Johnsen, the second engineer, had forty-five years of Arctic experience as an engineer and trader.

Five hours out, the pipes of the cooling system of the new engine began leaking. The *St. Roch* returned to the shipyard for repairs and left again on July 22. When she was well up the Nova Scotian coast, the engineers reported that the cooling system was still not working properly. Midmorning the following day someone smelled smoke. The deck around the exhaust was scorching and the seam pitch bubbling. The course was altered, and late in the afternoon the ship tied up at Sydney.

161

Except for the overheating problem, Larsen was more than satisfied with the engine's performance. Steaming the three hundred miles from Halifax, the *St. Roch* had averaged nearly nine knots. No one expected much extra speed because of the doubled horsepower. The hull wasn't shaped for it. The new engine would prove its worth when bucking wind and current and shoving floes aside. The ship could now force her way through packs that formerly would have stopped her dead.

In the morning naval personnel found the trouble to be improper ventilation. After repairs were completed a larger ventilator was installed, fuel and water tanks were filled, and the ship got under way again late afternoon of the twenty-sixth. For the past week the crew had enjoyed fine summer weather, but now they sailed into a thick fog and light rain. A few hours out in Cabot Strait the main clutch began to overheat, so they shut down and drifted until the trouble was found and corrected. The fog cleared before midnight, and they continued on at full revolutions.

The next evening whitecaps showed off South Head, Newfoundland. An easterly breeze, blowing from the Bay of Islands, was upsetting the sea. Entering the chop, the vessel began to plunge and take water over the forecastle. They took her in to Curling Cove for shelter. In the morning the fuel tanks were filled and Corporal Peters made more adjustments to the clutch. It caused no more trouble.

The *St. Roch* was at sea again at noon. The Gulf of St. Lawrence was calm and the weather clear. A few whitecaps still broke on the sparkling blue water, as clean as the puffs of cloud drifting high in the equally blue and sparkling sky. They were whiter than the sheep that grazed on the green slopes rising from the surf surging against the rocky western shore of Newfoundland. Black cattle and brown grazed there too, or rested under shade trees. An occasional team of horses pulled mowers or wagonloads of hay in fields set with red-roofed barns and white farmhouses.

There were no more problems with the engine, and the *St. Roch* made good time northward. She did not cruise alone. Boats and ships dotted the sea. Most were small, some with colored sails. Others, powered by chugging engines, came out from rocky coves and inlets bordered with villages as picturesque as their names—Chimney Cove, Cow's Head, Parson's Pond. White lighthouses marked prominent headlands and dangerous points.

Speedy destroyers and other naval vessels in dull war paint patrolled offshore and escorted convoys of merchantmen and tankers outbound for the North Atlantic. These were not sham exercises. The war had been carried here by Nazi U-boats. Allied vessels had been torpedoed on this shipping lane since the beginning of hostilities in 1939. A further reminder of the fighting three thousand miles away was the rumble of multi-engine bombers and transport planes passing overhead.

Following stepping-stone refueling bases on Newfoundland, Greenland, and Iceland enroute to Britain and Germany, the seldom seen but often heard aircraft used generally the same route as the Vikings who had reached the continent a thousand years before. Besides Iceland and Greenland, the old Norse sagas referred to Helluland, Markland, and Vinland. Scholars believed that Helluland, meaning "land of flat stones," was actually southern Baffin Island, and Markland, or "woodland," was probably Labrador. Vinland was known to be south of Markland, and most archaeologists agreed that it was actually Newfoundland, the island the *St. Roch* was at that moment passing.

The legends, customs and travels of the Norsemen were well known to Henry Larsen. Though he had been away from "the old country" for more than twenty years, had been a Canadian citizen for sixteen and rarely heard or spoke his mother tongue, he still thought much like a Norwegian. Even-tempered, methodical and practical, he was not especially imaginative. But it took little imagination

163

to see the ships of his blood-thirsty ancestors sailing down this same coast in search of plunder in their high-prowed, broad-beamed open boats.

The *St. Roch* passed steep mountains, fringed with timber on the skyline, slopes bearing scars where forests had been felled. "That reminds me of some of the places where the loggers have been along the British Columbia coast," Larsen said to the seaman at the wheel, a Nova Scotian bluenose.

"Have we much chance of getting there this year, Skipper?"

"I'm through making guesses, but if I were you, I'd take a good long look at all the trees and houses you can. You may not see anything but snow and ice for a long, long time."

The first ice was sighted in the Strait of Belle Isle on the morning of July 29, scattered bergs drifting off the southern coast of Labrador. Five hours after passing Red Bay at noon, the ship was in thick fog, running at half throttle. They had seen the last house and farm and village. Only foghorns on shore and the warning whistles of other vessels creeping through the overcast told them there were others than themselves in a world of gray mist and sea and abruptly looming icebergs. Larsen located and avoided the bergs the way he had navigated foggy channels on the West Coast—by blowing the whistle and listening for an echo. The growlers were a different matter, too low to return an echo. The lookout had to watch for them constantly.

The *St. Roch* sailed a course a few miles off the coast of Labrador, but because of the fog no land was sighted for four days. On the early morning of August 2, visibility improved enough for a headland to be sighted and identified as Cape Chidley at the entrance to Hudson Strait. Since leaving Halifax the ship had cruised 1,450 miles in 187 hours. The seven-and-a-half-knot average was encouraging.

The increasing ice and continuing fog was not. Besides

164

more and more bergs, the Labrador current was bringing pack ice from the north. By midday of August 3 it was so thick that even with the three-hundred-horsepower engine running at top speed the *St. Roch* made no progress. So Larsen ordered the engine shut down and they drifted. During the night the fog lifted for a time and the stars came out.

It was foggy again in the morning, but cleared enough to reveal that the coast of Baffin Island was packed with ice right to the shore. Giving up the plans to visit Frobisher Bay, Larsen began working eastward through the pack, toward the Greenland coast. The warmer West Greenland current flowing northerly from the Atlantic usually kept Davis Strait fairly ice-free this time of year.

Open water was seen ahead on the evening of August 4. They were clear of the ice at three in the morning, and by noon sheer mountains, topped by the Greenland Icecap, were visible across sunny seas from fifty miles offshore. Extremely large icebergs floated in the area, but they did not hinder navigation.

"I wish we didn't have to stop at Pond Inlet," Larsen said. "If we could keep going up the Greenland coast, we should have it good all the way to Lancaster Sound and not lose time working ice in Baffin Bay."

That afternoon he and the *St. Roch* crossed the Arctic Circle together for the thirteenth time. The following morning, off the Great Halibut Bank, he ordered the ship westward toward Baffin Island again. By late afternoon she made a landfall near the River Clyde. Soon they were in the pack again, shut down and drifting. On August 7 the sun shone long enough for a sextant sight to be taken. It showed that the gyrocompass had a twenty-five-degree easterly error.

Bylot Island was sighted on the ninth, but fog immediately shut out visibility and the *St. Roch* was moored to a floe to await clear weather. It didn't come until three mornings later. She got under way for Pond Inlet and dropped anchor there in the afternoon. The next day was Sunday, but the crew worked ten hours unloading supplies and coal for the R.C.M.P. detachment. On Monday, although a heavy surf made landing difficult, the remainder of the coal was put ashore and drums of oil brought out to the ship.

In anticipation of the ship's possibly becoming icebound, two native women were hired to make winter clothing for the crew. Also, arrangements were made with an Eskimo, Panipokachoo, to accompany the vessel and serve as guide and hunter if the voyage should not be completed in one season. He had no objection at all to traveling to Herschel Island, more than a thousand miles away, to make a new home in an unknown land. All that mattered was that his wife and mother, five children and seventeen dogs should go with him. They were brought aboard with their skiff and sled and other belongings. The dogs were tied on the main deck, and the family, declining cabin accommodations, set up a tent and stove atop the afterhouse. They settled down happily, looking forward to the voyage as the great adventure of their lives.

The *St. Roch*'s lightering scow and sleds and other trail equipment left at Pond Inlet two years before were reloaded and she sailed on the morning of August 17. A few hours out a stop was made at a native camp to pick up the rest of Panipokachoo's dogs and belongings. The ship continued north to Lancaster Sound by way of Eclipse Sound and Navy Board Inlet.

The young Eskimo mother's most valued possession was a hand-powered sewing machine. In fair weather she would sit on the main hatch stitching articles for her family and the crew. As she cranked material through the old machine, an alert baby in her parka watched over her shoulder. The older children played games in the skiff and scow amidships

166

and scrambled over the ship's gear and up the rigging while the dogs sprawled sleeping on the deck. The father, mechanically inclined like most Eskimos, spent most of his time in the engine room watching the machinery.

Lancaster Sound, the 250-mile-long channel extending from Baffin Bay to Barrow Strait, was the historic entrance to the Arctic. Into this channel explorers had sailed for hundreds of years searching for a Northwest Passage.

Except for occasional bergs, it was free of ice. The *St. Roch*'s first scheduled stop was to be at Devon Island on the north side of the sound. During the fifty-mile crossing a strong gale with snow blew out of the south. The absence of pack ice made the seas build up astern, and the ship rolled nastily until she reached the shelter of a big flat-topped iceberg adrift off Devon Island. Here she cruised to and fro, waiting for the wind to moderate. Even in the lee of the massive chunk of a glacier, freezing spray continually broke on board until she was sheathed in ice. Snug in their tent back aft, the Eskimos were comfortable. But their dogs, on top of the open deck load, suffered until the Mounties got them into the scow and covered it with canvas.

After six hours the weather calmed enough for the *St. Roch* to leave the iceberg and enter Dundas Harbour. The anchorage was exposed to a southerly swell kicked up by the gale, and the ship rolled heavily. A high surf pounded on the beach, but the crew managed a landing in a dory. The police buildings of a former R.C.M.P. detachment were inspected and found to be in good condition. Leaving a record of their visit in a brass cylinder, the shore party returned to the ship.

At four o'clock in the morning the *St. Roch* sailed into a freshening southeast wind. Hard rain and sleet made visibility poor, so she cruised slowly just off the high-cliffed shore. About noon, coming abeam a small opening in the cliffs, she entered and found a fair-sized inlet. Following it for several miles she anchored in a small cove. Here the Mounties went ashore again, built a cairn, and left another cylinder containing copies of the Northwest Territories ordinances and game regulations.

Reconnoitering the area, they saw many bear tracks, but no sign of other game. A small stream ran from the hills into the cove. On its bank they found the ruins of three Stone Age houses built of rock and bone. Larsen's explorer's instincts made him want to examine the region further, but during the night it began to snow. The wintry sign hurried them on.

Snow fell throughout the morning of August 20, limiting visibility as the *St. Roch* steamed along the southern coast of Devon Island. As she crossed Maxwell Bay, the weather cleared. Ahead, the cliffs of a high tableland rose straight up from the water without a sign of a beach. Cruising toward it, the ship reached Beechey Island in the afternoon and anchored in Erebus Bay. Named after one of Franklin's ships that had wintered here in 1845–1846 before sailing off to destruction, Erebus was one of the most historic harbors in the Canadian Arctic. Besides the Franklin expedition, several other explorers had made the narrow lowland at the foot of the cliff their winter quarters.

It was snowing lightly when the Mounties landed on Beechey Island in a dory. There was no doubt as to where they were. Broken barrels and thousands of staves littered the beach. The mast of a small vessel stood upright on the shore. However, they went first to a monument a few rods away on a pile of flat stones. An octagonal stone cenotaph about five feet high and topped by a sphere, it bore a plate to the memory of the members of the Franklin expedition and to those of the British Naval expedition under Sir Edward Belcher who perished in 1852 while searching for Franklin.

The mast and bits of stem and keel and planking were the

remnants of the twelve-ton yacht *Mary*. According to old records, she had been left at Cape Spencer by John Ross in 1850 in hopes that Franklin survivors might find her. Two years later, Commander Pullen of HMS *North Star* moved the vessel to Beechey Island. Captain Bernier, leader of the Canadian government expedition of 1908–1909, reported that he had found the yacht in good condition and pulled it up where ice and sea would not destroy it. How it came to be wrecked and who stuck the mast up on the beach was a mystery.

Not far from the remains of the *Mary* were five graves. Four were marked with weatherworn wooden headboards with the names of Franklin's men who had died here in early 1846. The other was unidentified. Nearby were the ruins of Northumberland House, a large stone cache built in 1954 by Pullen's men as a storehouse of supplies for vessels searching for the missing explorers. Little remained but the scattered staves and broken barrels.

A cairn on the plateau contained a record of Bernier's visit. The crew of the *St. Roch* added their own records. Finding nothing more of interest, they returned to the ship with some pieces of the keel and planking of the *Mary*.

Leaving the desolate, barren island, someone said, "If there's such a thing as ghosts, there sure would be some there."

They were glad to get away from Erebus Bay, haunted or not. The *St. Roch* had come nearly 3,000 miles from Halifax, but she was still 4,500 miles away from Vancouver, and the weather signs weren't good. For a time visibility was fair, but it began to diminish off Bathurst Island. With the gyrocompass in error and the near proximity of the north magnetic pole making the standard compass so erratic as to be useless, Larsen navigated Barrow Strait by all the tricks he knew.

He wrote: "We . . . passed Cape Hotham, Cornwallis

Island, and Wellington Channel which was clear of ice to the northward. But soon the weather changed, and eastward-drifting ice made its appearance. We by-passed Assistance Bay, and our course took us north of Griffiths, Somerville and Brown Islands through floes which, though all of this year's formation, kept getting heavier and more tightly packed. In these waters we bagged four walrus that provided a welcome change of food for us and supplemented the seal diet of the famished Eskimo dogs. At Cornwallis Island poor visibility and packed ice along the shore made landing unfeasible."

The pack was solid to the south, but open leads led westward toward Bathurst Island. At a point a few miles east of Cape Cockburn the *St. Roch* met pack ice riding a swift current down Austin Channel, which carried her twenty miles back to the east. She was finally able to break out and anchor behind grounded ice.

On the morning of August 24 a northwest wind cleared the ice from shore, and the ship got under way. Following the Bathurst coast to Cape Cockburn, she again anchored and a party went ashore. Captain Bernier claimed to have built a cairn there, but the Mounties couldn't find it. Because of the many bear tracks in the snow they assumed that the animals had destroyed it. To hold their container of records, they built their own cairn close to a conspicuous rock three hundred feet above the beach at the cape. Inland the island was covered with fresh snow.

[16]

"ICE PRESSURE FROM AUSTIN CHANNEL made it imperative that the vessel be moved without delay, so we weighed anchor at once and started working our way slowly northward. Though the surface looked broken here and there, it was solid; the constant southwest winds and heavy snowfalls held it tightly together. The weather was calm but visibility became so poor by five o'clock in the afternoon that we had to shut down. Later we tried several short leads but when they closed up we again stopped the engine and drifted in Graham Moore Bay."

Early on the morning of August 25 more leads opened, and the *St. Roch* began working through broken ice. A noon sight indicated her position to be nearly five hundred miles north of Cambridge Bay and eighteen hundred miles from Regina, Saskatchewan. It was the nearest to the Pole the ship had ever been.

During the evening fog rolled in, but Larsen found a good westward lead and followed it for several hours. At nine o'clock when the weather cleared, they sighted Byam Martin Island and anchored off its northeast point. In the morning Corporal Hunt took a party ashore and they dug through the deep snow for stones to build a cairn for the documents.

The *St. Roch* left the anchorage in beautifully clear

weather the same morning. There was little ice in Byam Channel, and she quickly crossed it. On Melville Island, twelve shaggy musk-oxen grazed near the beach. Westward, several more small herds of the hardy wild cattle appeared as the vessel cruised just offshore. In early afternoon what appeared to be a large cairn was seen inland. The ship anchored, and Hunt took a boat crew ashore to investigate. After walking about a mile and a half, they found the object to be a lone bull musk-ox standing motionless. They built a cairn there and left the records.

The ship got under way again at six P.M. of the twenty-sixth. The weather thickened in the evening, and when she anchored after midnight off Palmer Point it was snowing heavily. A party landed and deposited records in a pyramidal rock pile. Such pyramids, commonly built by Eskimos to stalk game behind, were evidence that the region had once been inhabited. In the afternon the weather cleared and the *St. Roch* departed for Dealey Island.

While she was still miles away, and the island itself was still below the horizon, a marker showed. Through binoculars it was identified as three barrels, one above the other, atop a spar mounted on a pile of stones on the highest point. The crew of HMS *Resolute,* commanded by Captain Henry Kellett, had built the cairn and set up the spar and barrels in 1852–1853 while on a Franklin search.

Anchoring close to the beach, the Mounties went ashore to mingle with more ghosts. A big stone cache, built in the shape of a house by Kellett's men, had been partially destroyed and the contents scattered around. Most of the walls were still intact, but the roof had fallen in. Outside, they found leather seaboots and broken barrels of spoiled peas and beans, tea, and chocolate. The skeletons of two bears were nearby. "Probably poisoned by eating rotten food," Hunt said.

Larsen looked around at the destruction of the cache.

"Bears didn't chop these barrels open—unless they had axes."

"Do you suppose Eskimos did it?"

"This isn't the work of natives. It was probably white men looking for grog."

"When I was here with Stefansson in 1917," Andreasen said, "at least a third of the cache was still usable."

It was later learned from official reports that Inspector A. H. Joy, R.C.M.P., on patrol from Dundas Harbour in 1929, had shot two bears at the cache, which probably accounted for the skeletons.

At one end of the cache were iron tanks that had rusted through. The hardtack in them was wet and soggy. Part of one wall was made of cases of canned meat and vegetables piled up and covered with sod. The central area of the structure was a mess of rotting clothing, broken barrels of flour and coal, rope, and ship's pulley blocks.

On the beach were two broken rifles and boxes of ammunition partly buried in the sand. Captain Bernier had left the weapons and cartridges here in 1909. The crew of the *St. Roch* salvaged a few articles of footwear, clothing, and the guns, as well as a few good tins of food for later analysis. One, containing ox cheek soup, still bore a label with the name of a manufacturer located near East India House in London. Directions for opening were: "Cut out one end with hammer and chisel. Use care to not let paint on can get into soup."

The cairn on top of the island contained a record left by Bernier. The Mounties took it with them and left their own. On the morning of August 28 the *St. Roch* left Dealey Island for Winter Harbour, thirty miles to the west. She anchored a few hours later in the bay where Lt. William E. Parry had wintered the *Hecla* and *Griper* in 1819–1820.

To stimulate exploration, in 1818 the British government had offered a prize of twenty thousand pounds to anyone who navigated the Northwest Passage, and five thousand pounds to reach the 110 meridian of west longitude. This point was at Cape Bounty, halfway between Dealey Island and Winter Harbour. In 1819 the British Admiralty had organized an Arctic expedition with Parry in command. Entering Lancaster Sound from Baffin Bay, he had found favorable ice conditions and continued westward, discovering Prince Regent Inlet, Barrow Strait, and Melville Sound.

Going ashore through chunks of drifting ice, the *St. Roch*'s men visited Parry Rock where the names "Hecla" and "Griper" had been carved by Parry's crew, with several of their own names.

"Parry was about the best of the Arctic explorers of those days," Larsen said. "We know how tough it was to get this far even with a good diesel engine. He did it with two sailing ships. If he'd kept going another week, he might have made the Northwest Passage. A few years after he was here he worked a ship into the pack to within seven and a half degrees of the Pole. That took seamanship!"

On the rock was a copper plate etched with the Union Jack and the Canadian coat of arms and an inscription:

"THIS MEMORIAL IS ERECTED TODAY TO COMMEMORATE THE TAKING POSSESSION FOR THE DOMINION OF CANADA, OF THE WHOLE ARCTIC ARCHIPELAGO, LAYING TO THE NORTH OF AMERICA. FROM LONG. 60 W. TO 141 W., UP TO LAT. 90 NORTH, WINTER HRB., MELVILLE ISLAND, C.G.S. ARCTIC. JULY 1ST, 1909, J. E. BERNIER, COMMANDER, J. V. KOENIG, SCULPTOR."

No records were found at Parry Rock, but in a small storehouse built by Bernier a bottle was hanging from a rafter. It contained a note left by Inspector Joy in 1929 while making the longest and most famous Arctic patrol in Mounted

Police history. The door of the house had been torn off. Except for a weather-ruined rifle and shotgun and a few rusted tins of tea and flour, it was empty. They took Joy's note to send back to Ottawa.

The weather was bad all day August 29, and the *St. Roch* remained at Winter Harbour preparing to cross Melville Sound when visibility improved. The fresh water was getting low in the tanks. Most of the streams ashore were dry. It took a boat crew two and a half hours to fill two barrels from a small creek. "I guess we'll have to go to the pack for water, Skipper," they said when they returned.

The weather cleared on the morning of the thirtieth and the *St. Roch* left at noon. The sea was open to the southwest, but ice showed on the horizon. She logged good time for the first hour, then slowed when fog set in. It lifted at five o'clock and the pack was dead ahead. Mooring to a floe, the crew filled the water tanks from a pond on the ice.

Early in the morning the ship began ramming through the ice in a mist and light rain. In sight of Banks Island she encountered the heaviest ice of the voyage when a west wind began pushing the Arctic Ocean pack down M'Clure Strait. At one o'clock the entrance to Prince of Wales Strait was in sight. Larsen intended to follow the passage to Amundsen Gulf, but a barrier of ice lay in between.

"At eleven a.m. on September 1 we tried a small lead but it soon petered out and we started drifting before a light north wind. The only ice movement was slow counter-clockwise revolutions in which we were locked until early afternoon of the following day. As visibility improved we resumed our southward grind. When land suddenly loomed ahead we were again forced to moor to ice grounded close to shore and await better weather, for, because of our merry-go-round drift, I couldn't decide whether we were near Russell Point on Banks Island or Peel Point on Victoria Island. . . . It was evident that the ice there [Melville Sound] had not

175

been subjected to great pressure, or been broken very long, for the sound was jammed with great heavy floes whose edges were sharp and straight, and some of the leads were so narrow that we had had difficulty squeezing through them.

"On September 3 we continued up what proved to be Richard Collinson Inlet, but as it was blocked with a great accumulation of ice with more pouring in from the sea behind us we made our way back along the coast line and around Peel Point into Prince of Wales Strait. There was very little ice here—only a few small pieces clinging to Banks Island—and the sun came out clear and bright to make it the best day of our entire trip. . . . We made good time until an hour before midnight when, due to darkness, we shut down and let her drift. We got under way again about 2 a.m., and as we passed Ramsay Island I noticed that the waters to the west were crammed with heavy ice and that the sky looked unfavorable. Threading through scattered floes, but favoured with good leads, we steamed past ice-packed Walker Bay, where we had wintered in 1940–41, and went on to Holman Island in the Western Arctic.

"Restfully, the *St. Roch* rode at anchor—as though catching her breath after her gallant victory over the Arctic maelstrom. It was mid-afternoon of Sept. 4, 1944. For the first time the northern route of the North-west Passage had been traversed.

"I thought it strange that no one came to meet us as Holman has a Hudson's Bay Co. trading post and a Roman Catholic mission. A blast from our air whistle brought signs of life, however, and ashore we learned that the people had been up all night unloading supplies from the H.B.C. M.S. *Fort Ross*, which had left only a few hours before our arrival, and tired out, they had been in bed. When awakened by our whistle they thought the *Fort Ross* had returned for some reason. Their explanatory greetings solved the riddle

176

of the slumbering islanders and told of another thing—the two ships had circumnavigated North America. The *Fort Ross* had left Halifax three months before we had and sailed through the Panama Canal, up the west coat. Subsequently we were to meet her at Tuktoyaktuk where she remained for the winter.

"Later I received instructions over the . . . wireless from the Commissioner to proceed to Vancouver, if feasible, and complete the coast-to-coast voyage."

The *St. Roch* spent the night at Holman Island and got under way again on the morning of September 5. The standard compass was still erratic, but the gyro had corrected itself and was dependable. A course due west would have taken the vessel to Cape Bathurst, the northernmost projection of the Western Arctic mainland. However, the easterly drift of ice through Amundsen Gulf forced her to follow a southwest bearing. By midnight, in an ice field twenty miles north of Keats Point, she shut down and drifted.

At four A.M., bucking a strong southwesterly wind, she began inching along the coast through pack ice. Rounding Cape Parry, she headed across Franklin Bay, buffeted by wind and ice. At times she was completely stopped, surrounded by the pack. "Wouldn't it be awful to come this far and get stuck, Skipper?"

"I've been frozen in, in worse places." Larsen pointed to the south. "We're not far from Langton Bay where we first wintered in '28."

Working to the western shore of Franklin Bay, the ship continued up the coast and anchored early in the evening in the shelter of Cape Bathurst. At four in the morning a snowstorm blowing off the land made it impossible to see, but she continued on, taking constant soundings. She crept along all day, inshore of the pack, until evening, when the way ahead was blocked. She moored to grounded ice off Toker Point near the Mackenzie delta.

177

The weather was thick all night but started to clear in midmorning. The ice was packed solidly seaward and to the west, with north winds driving more against the shore. Southwest there was a stretch of water kept open by a current from the river. At two in the afternoon the *St. Roch* started toward Tuktoyaktuk, reaching the harbor entrance at six. Unable to find the channel markers in the darkness, she ran aground. She backed off and anchored in deep water for the night.

"The morning of September 9 brought a gale and pouring rain. The heavy swell and shallow water made putting out to sea a risky undertaking, so with much difficulty we retreated to a sheltered spot in the harbour, dropped both anchors, each with 75 fathoms of chain, and waited for the blow that I knew was coming.

"And it came! The gale reached hurricane proportions and the water rose 10 ft. flooding the Hudson's Bay Co. buildings, washing away goods and equipment, and drowning several native-owned dogs. Small islands of peaty land embedded with willows and cranberry bushes swirled about in the rampaging waters. It was the worst storm that ever struck the settlement. The *St. Roch* rode it out but she had entered the harbour no more than in time to save herself from certain destruction.

"On September 10 when we managed to get ashore the sand-spit was completely changed, huge chunks of soil having been torn from its banks; old blue ice protruded everywhere, and Mackenzie Bay was turned into a solid mass of packed ice. We replaced the markers which had been blown down, and helped clear away the debris."

The weather continued bad with heavy rain and snow. While the *St. Roch* remained at anchor off Tuk Tuk, the crew sounded the channel from a dory and put up new markers. They were prepared to leave whenever a favorable wind started moving the pack away from shore. Things didn't look good. Point Barrow reported ice solid against the land—conditions the worst in many years. A plane flew in from Aklavik with an R.C.M.P. corporal who said that ice conditions were bad all along the coast. When the plane had gone, Larsen said, "I guess we can forget about getting home this year, boys," They set nets to catch fish for dog feed and examined the shore to find a good place for landing coal and supplies.

The skipper didn't care to winter at Tuktoyaktuk because of its stormy reputation and exposure to the north. On the morning of September 17, the weather cleared and a northeast wind began to move the ice.

"Let's get the anchor up," Larsen ordered. "Maybe we can make it to Herschel!" The hurricane waves had left the entrance even shallower than when they had entered, and the vessel grounded for a few minutes upon leaving. Once away from the shoals she made fair time. Taking advantage of the good weather, she cruised all day and through the night down leads that seemed to open just to help them on their way.

At dawn they were slowed by ice again, but found a long lead aimed right at Herschel Island. They passed unbroken floes ten miles long. One had seven bears on it, but no one was in a mood for hunting. Late in the day they entered the harbor and moored to the beach. The bay was filled with heavy, grounded ice from the previous winter, and the island wore a mantle of new snow. The crew set to work unloading fuel drums, gasoline, and kerosine.

The *St. Roch* had reached Herschel Island just in time. During the night a wild snowstorm drove in off the Beaufort Sea. The next day they were unable to unload or even leave the ship. Working in the hold sorting cargo, one of the seamen said: "The old man takes some awful chances with the weather, but it always seems to turn out all right. He's sure been lucky."

"He's not a bit lucky and he doesn't take chances," Corporal Hunt said. "He waits until the odds are with him and then he goes. In the years I've been with him he's hardly ever guessed wrong."

In the chart room, the "old man" was bringing his figures up to date. He'd brought the *St. Roch* 4,019 miles from Halifax in sixty-two days.

In the morning the temperature was 26° and the bay had a skim of new ice. The wind still blew from the northwest, but unloading continued and supplies were cached in an empty R.C.M.P. warehouse. There was no detachment here now or any natives, and with no extra help available cargo-handling was slow and tedious. However, with snow on the beach Panipokachoo's dogs could pull loads directly from ship to warehouse.

In the afternoon the sky cleared, and a brilliant sun came out. His weather sense alerted, Larsen said, "If it keeps getting better, we might get out of here after all." The crew needed no urging to hurry. Panipokachoo and his family were moved to a vacant house ashore, given a year's supplies and eleven tons of coal. They could live there comfortably until they were picked up again and taken to a place where they could return to Pond Inlet.

The weather improved all through the night. The wind was still out of the west on the morning of the twenty-first, but there was only scattered ice on the sea. The wireless operator again contacted Point Barrow. The pack was still against the shore there.

Early in the afternoon the west wind died. It was calm for a time, then light airs from the east began to ruffle the water. "We're getting out of here! Knock off that unloading and cover the hatch!" Larsen alerted the engineers with a clang of the telegraph gong as he moved the pointer to "Stand By."

The hatch was covered and battened. Mooring lines and the anchor were taken in. The crew called good-bys to "their family" on the beach. By midnight the *St. Roch* was fifty miles west of Herschel Island, working scattered ice.

The wind switched back to the west in the night, bringing thick, dark weather and ice from the Beaufort Sea. The pack seemed to do everything in its bag of evil tricks to impede the *St. Roch,* but the skipper had a few tricks of his own. Like a chess player, for every move the ice made, he had a countermove. Patience was his strongest weapon. If he waited long enough, eventually the ice would move. And he had power now to take advantage of the errors of his opponent. He would not be checkmated.

Off Camden Bay the weather cleared, and the *St. Roch* ran eight hours at full throttle through an iceless sea. In the evening fog rolled in, and she continued through a pitch-dark night at half speed, constantly sounding.

Just after midnight of September 24, Larsen was standing in the blacked-out wheelhouse, peering into the mist and listening to the leadsman calling soundings. He heard the splash of the lead, a long silence, then the cry, "We've lost the bottom!"

The skipper grinned. "We've passed the point. Full ahead!"

There was little fog west of Barrow, and soon he saw the lights of the settlement. He would have liked to stop, but ice was moving inshore. Bucking floes all morning, they left the pack behind at Wainwright.

The *St. Roch* recrossed the Arctic Circle, went through Bering Strait, and anchored off the King Island cliffs on the evening of the twenty-seventh. Wisps of smoke came from the chimneys of the shacks, but there was no sign of life. The whistle was blown, but it only disturbed the birds in the rookery. "They usually come out to sell souvenirs," Larsen said.

"Maybe they don't recognize the blue ensign, Skipper. There's a war on out here too, you know."

"So there is." The Stars and Stripes were hoisted, and the

village came to life. People poured from the houses, scurried down the flimsy ladders to the water, and launched their umiaks. Soon a dozen were aboard with walrus ivory carvings, miniature kayaks, cribbage boards, and other knick-knacks to trade for tobacco, tea, sugar, and such white man's fare as wartime isolation had deprived them of.

"Why did you hide when we showed up?" they were asked.

"We thought you might be Japs." With dark skins and Oriental features, the King Islanders themselves could have been mistaken for the enemy.

After several hours of visiting and bartering, the Mounties left the remote island of the cliff-dwelling ivory carvers. For most of the southward voyage down the usually stormy Bering Sea, they were blessed with fair weather. The jib and foresail were used, and the ship averaged eight knots throughout the three-and-a-half-day passage to the Aleutians.

They saw their first ship since leaving the Atlantic just after midnight of October 1—a large freighter heading north. Akutan Island was sighted at four o'clock, then the *St. Roch* met her old foe again—thick fog and dirty weather. She shut down and drifted, rolling heavily, until daylight. Navigating down the channel at slow speed, she entered Akutan Harbor and anchored off the U.S. Naval Fuel Base at the whaling station.

The whale fishery was shut down because of the war, but the odor of past operations still remained. "Probably smells no worse than I do," Larsen said. He hadn't slept without his clothes since leaving Sydney, Nova Scotia, seventy days before.

They were invited to moor to the pier and share the Navy's facilities. "Is there anything we can do for you, Captain?" the commander asked.

"Could we take baths?"

"You bet you can."

The long, hot showers, without concern for wasting precious water, were enjoyed even more than the dinner and movie that followed.

"The last time I ate in this mess hall," Larsen told the the senior officer, "we had whale steaks."

"Ugh! I hope they tasted better than they smell."

"That they did, and very good they were."

Bad weather kept them at Akutan until the fourth. While in port they took on diesel oil and filled the empty drums in the hold with ballast. Sailing at one o'clock, the *St. Roch* rounded Akun Head an hour and a half later and entered Unimak Pass. The wind was westerly, the swell was heavy, and visibility was cut by rain squalls. The ship reached the Pacific at half past six. The weather remained poor until midnight, then began to clear with each mile she moved away from the Aleutians.

The sails were set, and the vessel made 200 miles on the fifth of October, 207 on the sixth, and the same the next day. On Sunday morning the pleasant southerly turned into a gale, and the *St. Roch* began to roll and ship water. She was hove to with engine turning slowly, and pitched and rolled all night long. In the morning she continued on course with sails reefed and engine at half speed. The wind moderated in the afternoon, but the swell continued to be heavy and only sixty miles were logged that day. On the tenth the wind was still strong and the sea rough, but engine speed was increased and the ship covered 148 miles.

The eleventh dawned clear and calm, and the *St. Roch* plunged along, homeward bound at eight knots. The Queen Charlotte Islands hove up over the rim of the ocean at six in the morning and by midnight the Mountie ship was abeam St. James Light. She entered the Inside Passage on October 12 and anchored for the night in Shushortie Bay. Larsen made his daily calculations. "We've come 7,022 miles from Halifax, and we're 250 miles from Vancouver. It's all over but the shouting, boys!"

Thick autumn fogs all along the Inside Passage slowed the *St. Roch*. It took her four days to reach Vancouver. Entering the First Narrows eighty-six days after leaving Halifax, she tied up at the Evans, Coleman & Evans wharf at six P.M. of October 16. All her flags were flying, and she carried in the rigging a white banner showing the buffalo emblem of the R.C.M.P. and the lettering "N W PASSAGE."

It *was* all over but the shouting, and there was little, if any, of that. As far as the Force was concerned, the *St. Roch* was just another Mounted Police detachment returning to home base after quietly and efficiently completing its assigned duties in the prescribed manner.

Epilogue

THE SHOUTING came ten years later. On Columbus Day of 1954, escorted by police launches and private yachts, with helicopters buzzing overhead and the big white ice-breaker HMCS *Labrador* and others following respectfully astern, the *St. Roch* led a marine parade through the First Narrows. She had just completed her final voyage, coming home from Halifax by way of the Panama Canal with Superintendent Henry Larsen in command. The *Labrador* was being honored too, having just completed her first voyage through the Northwest Passage.

Outmoded by powerful icebreakers and transport planes, the *St. Roch* was too small and no longer practical for modern Arctic needs. Found decaying in an East Coast dockyard, she would have been sold as a fishing vessel or scrapped but for the City of Vancouver. Stung by shaming statements of the city archivist, Major J. S. Matthews, the city raised funds and bought her from the government for the cost of bringing her home—$5,000.

In ceremonies held on October 13, 1954, the *St. Roch* was officially presented to the City of Vancouver to become a national historic relic. At this time Henry Larsen returned to Major Matthews a weatherworn Union Jack the archivist had given to him years before. The *St. Roch* had flown it in the Arctic and from coast to coast and had carried it at her masthead when she had headed the parade the day before.

In 1954 the weary old vessel was displayed in connection with the British Empire Games held in Vancouver. In the summer of 1958 she was placed on permanent display in a drydock built especially for her at Kitsilano Beach. In May of 1962 the area was declared a national historic site. Housed in an attractive shelter, the restored *St. Roch* is now the principal exhibit of the Vancouver Maritime Museum.

Besides being the first vessel to complete the Northwest Passage from west to east, and the first to go the route in both directions, the *St. Roch* was also first to round the North American continent. In 1950, ordered to the East Coast for duty by way of Panama, she completed the circumnavigation upon reaching Halifax.

Historic relic indeed!

Henry Larsen received his share of the honors. In September of 1944 he was commissioned a sub-inspector of the R.C.M.P., was promoted to inspector in 1946, and became a superintendent in 1953. He was a Fellow of the Royal Canadian Geographical Society and a Fellow of the Arctic Institute of North America. In addition to the Silver Polar Medal awarded to him and the crew for the 1940–1942 voyage, in 1946 he was given the Gold Patron's Medal of the Royal Geographical Society of London.

In 1947 he became an Honorary Fellow of the Royal Geographical Society, and a year later was presented with the bar to his Polar Medal. He was first to receive the Massey Medal of the Canadian Geographical Society, presented in 1959. In May of 1961 he received the honorary degree of Doctor of Laws from Waterloo University College.

The Norwegian lad from Fredrikstad had come a long way.

He was a graduate of the Canadian Police College. From 1949 until his retirement on February 7, 1961, he was stationed at Ottawa as Officer Commanding "G" Division, R.C.M.P. His work there dealt with the Northwest Territories and the Yukon. During these years he made many visits, generally traveling by air, to his beloved Arctic in connection with official duties.

Following retirement, Larsen and his wife and their son Gordon and daughters Doreen and Beverley lived for a time at Lunenberg, Nova Scotia. Tiring of the East, they returned to Vancouver to make their home there. On October 29, 1964, following a short illness, Larsen died and was buried in the R.C.M.P. cemetery at Regina, Saskatchewan.

As of this writing, some of the crewmen who served with Larsen in the *St. Roch* are still around. Dad Parry, ship's cook and handyman for fourteen years, is living out his retirement in Victoria, British Columbia. Jack Foster, chief engineer for ten years, is in Vancouver. He and Siddie still see Mary Larsen. Anderton, Peters, Hunt, and others, all retired from the Force, live in the Vancouver area. Staff Sergeant John Friederich, still on active duty, heads the R.C.M.P. detachment that polices North Vancouver, not far from the shipyard where the *St. Roch* was built.

Honestly proud of his accomplishments, Henry Asbjorn Larsen never lost the humble touch of the common man. He had equaled and in some respects bettered the feats of his boyhood idol, Roald Amundsen, but retained his admiration for the great explorer. He tended to play down what he himself had done. After completing the second Northwest Passage Voyage, he said:

"We were lucky and had the breaks. No one can predict ice or navigation conditions in the Arctic. What we accomplished this year might be repeated the next, or it might be many years. Much would depend upon the type of vessel used and the ice conditions of that particular year. Our voyage showed that the Northwest Passage can be traversed in a single year, but does not prove that this could be accomplished every year."

Canada and the R.C.M.P. gave Henry Larsen the opportunity and the ship to pursue the career for which he was particularly trained and suited. In return he gave the best he had, which made him the greatest of Canadian Arctic navigators.

Bibliography

Kemp, Vernon A. M., *Without Fear, Favour or Affection.* Toronto: Longmans, Green & Co., 1958.

Larsen, Sergeant Henry A., *The North-West Passage: The Famous Voyages of the Royal Canadian Mounted Police Schooner "St. Roch."* Ottawa: Edmond Cloutier, Queen's Printer, 1958.

Phillips, Alan, *The Living Legend.* Little, Brown and Company, 1957.

Royal Canadian Mounted Police, 1945: Reports and Other Papers Relating to the Two Voyages of the R. C. M. Police Schooner "St. Roch." Ottawa: Department of Public Printing and Stationery, 1945.

R.C.M.P. Commissioner's Reports. Years ending Sept. 30, 1928, 1929, 1930, 1931, and 1932.

R.C.M.P. Quarterly, October, 1942, and April, 1945.

Robinson, J. Lewis, *Conquest of the Northwest Passage by R.C.M.P. Schooner "St. Roch."* Smithsonian Institution, Annual Report, year ended June 30, 1945. U.S. Government Printing Office, Publication 3817, pages 219–234.

Tranter, G., *Plowing the Arctic.* Toronto: Longmans, Green & Co., 1945.

Biography of Tom E. Clarke

Tom E. Clarke was born in the State of Washington. He still lives there, in Seattle, with his family, including two sons and a daughter.

From his mid-teen years he traveled the Northwest country, working as a ranch hand, truck driver, railroad worker, cook, deckhand—a jack-of-all-trades. He returned eventually to Sequim, Washington, and graduated from high school.

Serving in the U.S. Army during World War II, Clarke spent some time in Anchorage, Alaska. After his discharge from the Army he returned to Alaska as a deckhand on a cannery tender. From there he went on to attend business college in Seattle, Washington. During this time he became a court reporter. He later took courses in creative writing at the University of Washington in Seattle.

A qualified press photographer and free-lance writer, Tom Clarke has done feature writing for *The Seattle Times and Post Intelligencer*. His work has appeared in *Reader's Digest* and *Jack and Jill*. He is the author of five other books, adventure novels for the young adult.